Successful Independent Consulting

Relationships that Focus on Mutual Benefit

Johanna Rothman

Successful Independent Consulting

Relationships that Focus on Mutual Benefit

Johanna Rothman

Published by Practical Ink
www.jrothman.com

Practical **ink**

Cover design: Cathi Stevenson, BookCoverExpress

Ebook: 978-1-943487-28-8
Paper: 978-1-943487-29-5
Hardcover: 978-1-943487-30-1

For Mark and the rest of our family, as always.

"Johanna has packed this book with helpful advice and provocative questions to help you on your way to being a successful consultant. There's more in here than just getting started, however. I've been an independent consultant for close to two decades, and I find lots of advice that's helpful to me now. And I find provocative questions that help me think about where I want my consulting practice to go next. If you're consulting or considering consulting, I feel confident that you'll find plenty of value in this book."

—GEORGE DINWIDDIE, AUTHOR AND CONSULTANT

"In my 30+ years of consulting, I've read many getting 'started' books about client relationships and everything that goes into successful consulting. Johanna didn't stop there. She identifies the traps that seem good at the time but create uncomfortable and awkward situations. This book offers alternatives for what successful consultants can do instead. Read it, use it, and succeed on your own terms."

—DON GRAY, CONSULTANT AND CO-CREATOR OF THE GROWS METHOD®

"*Successful Independent Consulting* is both pragmatic and insightful. It helped me identify my blind spots and offered practical tips to improve what I was already doing. Highly recommended."

—JOANNE PEROLD, INDEPENDENT CONSULTANT AT FAETHM,
A BOUTIQUE CONSULTANCY

"Especially in lean times, it's not easy to become an independent consultant. Even great economic times don't guarantee anyone's consulting success. But if you think you'd like the rewards, such as fitting work to your life—not the other way around—*Successful Independent Consulting* is the book you need. Use the exercises to start, maintain, or even evolve your focus."

—WILLEM VAN DEN ENDE, INDEPENDENT CONSULTANT

Contents

PART I
Build Your Consulting Engine

PART **2**

Create and Maintain a Business That Works for You

Acknowledgments

I thank my consulting cohorts and reviewers for their review and comments: Ahmed Avais, Gil Broza, Rob Bowyer, Vladimir Bushin, Mun-Wai Chung, George Dinwiddie, Aanu Gopald, John Healy, Michael Hunter, Jon Jorgensen, Mark Kilby, Ryan Latta, Joe Lynch, Susan Moore, Brett Palmer, Kemmy Raji, Amitai Schleier, Lisa Sieverts, Daniel Steinberg, JF Unson, ShriKant Vashishta.

I thank Rebecca Airmet and Mark Posey for their editing. I thank Karen Billipp for her layout and Jean Jesensky for her indexing. I thank Cathi Stevenson from BookCoverExpress for her cover design.

Any mistakes are mine.

Introduction

I started 1994 as a middle manager in a software organization. In August of that year, I argued—politely—with a senior manager. Three weeks later, that company laid me off. My employer called it a layoff, but I was the only one affected.

I'd flirted with the idea of consulting before, but had not prepared for an abrupt transition to running my own business. It took me three months, but I landed a workshop as my first engagement in 1994. The next year, I replaced my salary. But, finally, in 1996, I made enough money as a consultant that my business was successful enough to more than replace my employee salary and benefits.

I've now spent almost three decades as an independent consultant.

Along the way, I've learned what's worked for many other successful independent consultants and me. Successful independent consultants share many of the same qualities. We practice these actions, what I refer to as the consulting engine:

- Use both consistent and a variety of content marketing to attract our ideal clients.
- Learn via formal and informal training throughout our consulting careers.
- Choose which work to do and when to drop certain work.
- Charge enough for our expertise so our clients see our value and we benefit.

In addition to the consulting engine, we create systems so our businesses can thrive.

If you're considering consulting, this book contains everything I know about how to be a successful independent consultant.

Maybe you've seen consultants who were not successful. In my experience, these consultants miss one or more of the consulting engine actions.

There are even some common sayings about consulting. Maybe you've heard, "Consultants are people who take your watch, tell you what time it is, and then charge you a pile of money." In this case, the client does not perceive any added value from the consultant. Too often, that's because the consultant does not have the expertise or experience to deliver value.

Or, you might have seen the consultant-as-seagull. They swoop around, poop a lot, and then leave. When they leave, the client is often in a worse place. In my experience, seagull consultants have expertise in a box. If the client needs their expertise, that's great. But the consultant doesn't have enough critical thinking skills or additional expertise or experience to deliver value to the client.

Worse, you might see a too-common practice of larger consulting firms. The senior people at the top of a consulting firm sell the services to the client. Then, the people at the "bottom," the new, untested, and inexperienced people, deliver the services. Without experience, these people stumble through engagements.

These consulting options all focus on the consultant's personal benefit, often doing something *to* the client. None of these options create win-win relationships for effective and mutual benefit.

Instead, successful independent consultants use their expertise, and all their value to build relationships and deliver results *with* their clients.

Consultants support a client's changes. Clients learn and grow. In exchange, clients pay consultants. However, successful independent consultants also learn from the engagement and gain more experience.

That relationship and learning—not only money—is how independent consultants succeed. It's also how they build relationships that can help the consultant serve that client again and again.

You don't have to resort to taking watches, acting like a seagull, or separating how you sell your services from delivering those services.

Instead, you can create a satisfying and successful professional life that serves you and your clients.

There are two parts to becoming a successful independent consultant: working *in* the business, to create your consulting engine, and working *on* the business, to maintain your sanity and excitement.

Let's start with the consulting engine.

PART 1

Build Your Consulting Engine

Many successful independent consultants describe an iterative loop for their business. These consultants:

- Based on the consultant's expertise, decide which problems they will help their clients solve.
- Attract clients with ongoing content marketing.
- Create relationships with not just the person who can buy their services, but with more people across the organization.
- Learn from the engagement. Should the consultant offer this kind of engagement again or modify it? Might the consultant look for more clients like this one or expand their potential client base? These reflections help the consultant recognize their increased value and which problems to solve next.

That's the consulting "engine."

Successful consultants iterate their way through the engine loop. Along the way, the consultant and client build and maintain a relationship based on trust and respect. Clients rarely receive the outcomes they want and need without that trust and respect.

This part of the book is how you can build your consulting engine, starting with how you might assess your current value to potential clients.

CHAPTER 1

Define Your Unique Value

Consultants start with specific expertise. The more you consult and build your content marketing, the more you'll iterate your practice, evolving it. Consider thinking about your successful consulting practice as a jewel, with multiple facets sparkling in any light. Your expertise creates those facets, as you choose how to offer your value to clients.

As an employee, your manager or organization might have limited where you could offer value. You had a role and fulfilled it.

As a consultant, you have the opportunity to see and experience more situations than most employees have. Assuming you learn from that experience, you can now provide more value to more kinds of organizations and people. The more you consult, the more valuable you become to your clients.

How can you tell where you add value? Consider anything you taught others. Or what people tell you is your "superpower."

You might add value because you have a different perspective or slant on your consulting topics.

That value exists because consultants help clients see what or how to change.

1.1 How Consultants Add Value to Clients

Consultants help a client transform or change in some way, to improve the client's condition. That means consultants can work in any number of roles to help the client improve.

The article, *Choosing a Consulting Role: Principles and Dynamics of Matching Role to Situation* CKM90, describes possible roles and stances we might take as consultants.

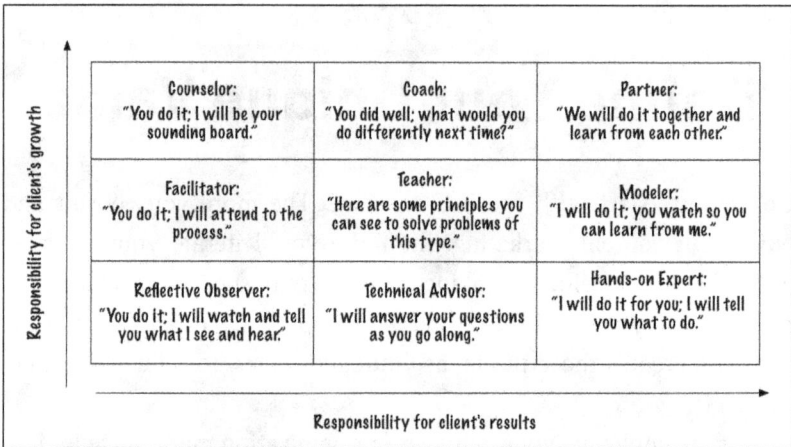

Counselor: "You do it; I will be your sounding board."	**Coach:** "You did well; what would you do differently next time?"	**Partner:** "We will do it together and learn from each other."
Facilitator: "You do it; I will attend to the process."	**Teacher:** "Here are some principles you can see to solve problems of this type."	**Modeler:** "I will do it; you watch so you can learn from me."
Reflective Observer: "You do it; I will watch and tell you what I see and hear."	**Technical Advisor:** "I will answer your questions as you go along."	**Hands-on Expert:** "I will do it for you; I will tell you what to do."

Responsibility for client's growth (vertical axis)

Responsibility for client's results (horizontal axis)

Figure 1.1: Possible Consulting Roles

The more consultants facilitate the client's work, the more valuable the consultant is to the client. The upper rows and leftmost columns are more facilitative roles. Consultants can charge more for that kind of work.

Here are some examples of how consultants differ from employees.

As an employee, Andrea, a senior software developer, already works as a Technical Advisor, Modeler, and Hands-on Expert. She knows she can perform those roles as a consultant. However, she wants to add Teacher, Coach, and Partner to her skills to succeed as a consultant. For that, she will need to improve her communication and relationship skills.

Simon, originally an employee project manager, stopped managing projects as a Hands-On Expert several years ago. Now, as a consultant, he uses his project management background to set agendas and teach others how to facilitate all kinds of meetings and workshops. He has added Teacher, Coach, and Counselor to his skills.

The more responsibility you have for the client's growth, the more value you offer as a consultant.

That's why successful consultants review their skills periodically to see where they offer value to their clients.

Aside from your perspective or slant on your expertise, clients buy your services so you can support their desired changes. (Some clients don't want to change, but you might only learn that once you're in the engagement. See Strengthen the Client Relationship (p. 137) for details about this and other client problems during an engagement.)

1.2 Understand Your Skills

If you're new to consulting, consider these questions to frame your thinking:

- You excelled at some of your past work, and you know other companies (or people) will pay for that work.
- People asked you for advice based on your work.
- Somebody said, "You should be a consultant because you offered me so much value when you did this thing for us."

Your client value is your perspective plus your interpersonal skills.

Think back to what other people asked you to do—or that you volunteered to do—because you're good at those activities. If most of your skills, similar to Andrea's in the previous section, lie primarily in the how-to-do-the-work, use the ideas in Appendix A: Evaluate Your Technical Skills (p. 253) to inventory them.

But don't stop with technical skills. While technical skills can be quite useful, they are not sufficient for long-term success. That's because the more a consultant has responsibility for the client's growth and results, the more the consultant will facilitate other people's work.

That facilitation often starts with communication skills.

1.2.1 *Communication Skills*

Brian, an experienced software architect, told me that he worked with highly technical teams, day in and day out. He also said: "The more I practice my interpersonal skills, the feedback, coaching, and influence, the more successful I am as a consultant."

That's because, as Gerald M. Weinberg said in *The Secrets of Consulting: A Guide to Giving and Getting Advice Successfully* WCO14:

"*No matter how it looks at first, it's always a people problem.*"

Your technical skills might help you sell an engagement. However, your interpersonal skills will help you propose and deliver a successful engagement. Interpersonal skills help consultants describe and communicate how the client's environment aids or prevents them from seeing their challenges or changing.

Here are some communication skills most consultants need to be successful:

- Asking open-ended questions and using active listening to hear the answers.
- Writing, speaking, and visualizing what you see so clients can understand their current challenges.
- Writing, speaking, and visualizing your work as content marketing to attract more clients.

All these skills require empathy with your clients and where they are in their change journey. That leads to effective relationship-building with your clients.

1.2.2 *Relationship-Building or Influencing Skills*

Only one of the consulting roles, the Hands-on Expert, in Figure 1.1: Possible Consulting Roles (p. 4) allows the consultant to deliver outcomes alone. All the other roles require interactions with the client.

Successful independent consultants build relationships with many people at a given client—especially the person who signed the Purchase Order. (See Recognize Your Buyer on p. 71 to understand the various roles the client personnel might take.)

Here are some necessary relationship-building skills:

- Build rapport with potential and current clients, especially with the economic buyer. That rapport allows consultants to retain the client for more engagements.
- Build trust with potential and current clients.
- Maintain sufficient self-esteem, so the consultant doesn't need to take credit for their client's successes.
- Focus on outcomes. Sometimes, consultants are attached to a specific process or tool, especially if the consultant offers a certification or is part of a certification system. When consultants focus on outcomes, they can offer their clients several options to achieve their desired changes.

The more you build these relationship-oriented skills, the more success you will have in influencing clients to consider and use the changes you recommend. (Influence includes exploring what the client might want as results and how they might achieve those results.)

You don't need all of these skills *right now*. You can practice and learn them as you proceed. However, successful consultants have enough of these skills to offer sufficient value to their clients.

Many successful consultants also share these personal qualities.

1.2.3 *Personal Qualities*

Our qualities help us build client relationships. Here are qualities I have found helpful:

- Initiative. You take the initiative to get clients, get referrals, and do the necessary work to succeed in an engagement.
- Curiosity. The more curiosity you have, the more likely you are to learn more and keep an open mind about your clients and their challenges.
- Adaptability. You can consider several options for many situations.
- Resilience. You can recover from setbacks.
- Perseverance. You don't quit. You have sufficient grit.

- Collaborative. You're willing to work with your client.
- Negotiation. Find ways to create win-win situations. You will need these skills to create engagements and deliver the desired outcomes.
- Influence. You can exhibit your competence and build rapport to assist others in considering and implementing their possible choices.

While each consultant has more or less of each of these qualities, most successful consultants also find ways to build rapport with potential clients quickly.

Some people call these "soft" skills. I prefer to call them interpersonal skills. Ask yourself which of these skills you want to practice to influence others and create a resilient business.

As you use your communication skills to strengthen relationships with the client, you might need to learn how to explain the client's challenges. Those are critical thinking skills.

1.2.4 *Critical Thinking Skills*

While clients often see the problem signals, clients don't always see the root cause(s) of their problems. Worse, clients don't always recognize the range of reasonable solutions for those problems.

Successful consultants will support the client as the client learns to see their challenges. Many consultants use a variety of critical thinking tools to help explain the situation and create options for change.

Here are some possible critical thinking skills tools:

- Force Field Analysis
- Causal loop diagrams with reinforcing and balancing feedback loops.
- Several kinds of data collection and organization, both qualitative and quantitative. For example, I've calculated cycle time, Cost of Delay, and the effects of delayed customer response times for different clients.

Avoid accepting the very first root cause you see. Remember to look for indications of much deeper problems.

For example, value stream mapping helps me explain the effects of people working separately. However, the map alone does not help the client reason about the situation.

Consider when you will review the various models and lenses you use. Sometimes, the client needs a different lens on the situation. See Consider These Consulting Tools (p. 257) for more ideas.

The more you consider different ways to explain the client's challenges and possible options for solutions, the more you will hone your critical thinking tools.

Even if the client only pays lip service to change, your client deserves your best reasoning about what you see and their options.

1.3 Inventory Your Skills

Take time to assess your consulting-specific skills. Figure 1.2, Skills Inventory Worksheet, on page 10 is a worksheet also has the more traditional skills from Appendix A: Evaluate Your Technical Skills (p. 253):

You don't need skills in all areas—you can only maintain skills in some areas. However, consider which functional and consulting skills offer the most value to your clients. Then, you decide which other skills you might choose to acquire.

Everyone is unique. And, as long as you Keep Learning (p.209), you'll continue to add to your skills.

Now, it's time to see how you've used those skills in the past. What you've learned so far offers value to your potential clients.

1.4 Articulate Your Value

How will *you* support your clients to see their possibilities and guide them through their changes? Remember the roles from Figure 1.1: Possible Consulting Roles (p. 4).

Do you need to compete with all the other consultants in your field?

Consider which skills you want to from Appendix A: Functional skills Problem domain expertise Tools and technology, Industry expertise	
Communication Skills	
Personal Qualities	
Relationship-building	
Critical thinking	
Any other skills you think will offer your clients specific value	

Figure 1.2: Skills Inventory Worksheet

No, for two reasons.

First, you offer specific, unique value. How will *you* help your clients improve and change? What's different about what you can offer your clients? That's the combination of your perspective and your experience.

Second, successful independent consultants can experiment and evolve their practices on purpose. You don't have to "scale" your business to succeed, so you don't have to compete with other consultants.

If you wonder about your unique value, think back to how you've succeeded through the years.

One way to do this is to review your previous work and assess the tangible and intangible benefits of that work to your previous employers or clients. You might discover that you offer more value than you think you do.

Here's how to start:

1. For each recent role, either as a consultant or an employee, list your actions with verbs. Did you facilitate, teach, lead, or perform some other action? Write down everything for that role.

2. Determine your tangible value. Your actions helped the company save money or time, increase revenue, or something else of value to the client. Estimate the monetary value of your work.

3. Assess your intangible value. Your actions might have: helped a team work better together, created better relationships, or facilitated other people's actions.

Remember to add what your boss or client said about your value.

The combination of your actions, plus your tangible and intangible value, will help you see how to define your value.

1.5 Assess Previous Work

Whether you worked as an employee or consultant, assess your previous work to see how you increased which skills. Consider the table in Figure 1.3, Consulting Performance Against Value (p. 12) to assess your work quarterly or yearly:

If you're assessing your employee work, consider how that work can map to consulting engagements. Ask these questions as you evaluate the results:

- Start with column 1, the engagement. What is your assessment of the success of that engagement? (Put each engagement into one of the Successful, In Progress, or Unsuccessful rows.)
- In column 2, assess the client value. What kind of value did the client receive? Even engagements In Progress might offer some value so far.
- In column 3, assess the value you received.

Consider a separate page for each year of work, starting with the most recent year. Now you can decide if you want more or less of that

Consulting Performance Against Value			
Engagement	**Value to Client**	**Value to You**	
Successful engagements	List each successful engagement	List all the possible value the client received	
Engagements still in progress	List in progress engagements	Value so far	
Unsuccessful engagements	List each unsuccessful engagement	Even some unsuccessful engagements might offer value	

Figure 1.3: Consulting Performance Against Value

kind of work. Then determine if you will change your skills to increase your client's success or value.

That's when you might choose which skills to reinforce—or release.

1.6 Choose Which Skills To Reinforce

Which skills do you want to reinforce or acquire? I've offered several ways to think about skills.

Ask this question:

Do you have sufficient skills to do the consulting you want to do?

Long ago, I met John, who'd graduated from university three years earlier. His title at the time was "Senior Software Engineer."

He told me he wanted to consult as a software architect. I asked him this question:

"What three systems have you architected, either as a lead or as part of the architecture effort?"

He frowned. "None," he said. "How hard can it be? The architects are wrong, anyway. They get paid a lot."

I asked him if he wanted feedback. John did. I suggested he might not have considered all relevant aspects of consulting:

1. Clients only pay you if you can help them change or solve their problems. If you don't have the experience to do the job, the clients will learn that and fire you.
2. What previous successes would allow him to obtain an engagement?
3. Did he plan to acquire all his expertise while consulting for his clients? If he was honest with clients, that might be okay. Did he want that career path?

We discussed the value of living with our design, code, and tests for several years to see how our early decisions affected later possibilities.

He hadn't thought of any of that. He thought consulting was straightforward and offered easy money. John didn't consider his potential value to the client or ongoing work from the client.

The deeper your skills—in your chosen dimensions—the more effective you can be as a consultant. Deep experience can help you find better clients. Because you offer more value, you can ask for and receive higher fees.

Use your skills inventory to see when it makes sense to start or evolve your consulting business. See where you want more experience and decide how to get that experience.

As you assess your skills, remember to maintain your self-esteem.

1.7 Maintain Your Self-Esteem

Some consultants think they are above average and can solve "all" their clients' problems—an example of the Dunning-Kruger effect. The

Dunning-Kruger effect causes us to overestimate our abilities—that we are always above average. These people don't learn from feedback, which not only detracts—but short circuits—their learning from their experience.

On the other hand, some consultants suffer from Imposter Syndrome, where they worry if they have any capabilities at all and think they are a fraud. They might take "safe" engagements and avoid potential risks, experiments, and alternatives. They repeat the same year(s) of experience again and again.

Neither is a healthy state. And either state prevents consultants from learning.

Both Imposter Syndrome and Dunning-Kruger thinking can damage your self-esteem. Consultants need their self-esteem for everything they do.

Instead, consider the idea of the growth mindset from Carol Dweck's book *Mindset: The New Psychology of Success* DWE07. Dweck's book describes the fixed mindset and the growth mindset. When you have a fixed mindset, you think people have—or do not have—specific capabilities or skills. You might even call those skills talents.

When we use the growth mindset, we reframe our thinking into learning. Instead of assuming we have "natural" skills or talents, we choose to learn and practice almost anything.

One of the ways I build my self-esteem is to practice something every day. (See James Clear's *Atomic Habits* CLE18.)

In addition, consider reading Weinberg's *More Secrets of Consulting: The Consultant's Toolkit* WCM14. That book is about the self-esteem toolkit most consultants need throughout their careers.

1.8 Clarify the Value You Bring to Clients

Throughout this chapter, I've suggested ways you can think about the skills you bring to your potential clients. Now it's time to discuss what makes you a unique consultant.

You.

All of you, including your experience and perspectives, together in one package.

Until now, your managers might have offered you feedback to make you more like others. But sameness doesn't work for consultants. Successful independent consultants optimize for their uniqueness.

As a consultant, your first sale is to yourself. If you believe in your value, you can craft your marketing, proposals, and services to showcase your value to your clients.

1.9 Now Try This to Recognize Your Unique Value

Each chapter in this book has a "Now Try This section." You will gain the most from this book if you take the time to answer every chapter's questions. I recommend you use a notebook, whether it's electronic or physical.

In your consulting notebook, write down your answers to these questions:

1. Review your perspectives about the problems you want to solve with your clients. What about your perspective is different? If your perspective is the same as others, how will you make it different in some way?
2. What did you learn about yourself from your skills inventory? What surprised you about your current skills?
3. Which skills do you prefer to perform? Which skills do you want to adopt or learn as a challenge to yourself? Make an action plan now for the skills you want to learn.
4. Where has your work offered you and your client/employer the most value?

You know your expertise and value. Now it's time to move to how your skills match the problems you see and that your potential clients have.

CHAPTER 2

Identify Your Ideal Clients

Your skills, perspectives, and value can help you identify your ideal clients by their problems.

Successful independent consultants don't try to be everything to all possible clients. Instead, choose your ideal clients by selecting the problems you want to address.

You can choose almost any client problem and make it part of your business. However, the more specifically you describe what the client sees—the signals of the problem—the easier it will be for you to create a successful business.

Start by describing the signals in words your clients tend to use.

2.1 Describe the Signals Your Clients See

In my experience, many clients believe the signal they see is the problem. Sometimes, the client is correct—but only sometimes.

One consultant heard each of these statements from one client:

- A team lead said, "I can't get anything done between 9 and 5. We have too many meetings.
- A tester said, "I can't get anything done. I'm on too many projects."
- A manager said, "The team never gives me a date I can trust. But I need to give my manager a date for this work."
- A middle manager said, "I don't feel as if I'm making a difference. We do all this work, and we have nothing finished to show for it."

- A senior manager said, "I'm sure the department is wasting time. It can't take them this long to deliver something, can it?"

All these pain points—at different levels—in the same organization. One significant signal is that the organization multitasks on too much work in progress. But there are several intervention points, and different consultants will offer different support for the client's changes.

That's because every consultant decides which signals, or pain points, to address.

If you prefer to work with teams and people on teams, you might address the signals of too many meetings and too many projects. Alternatively, you could work with only the managers who focus on tactical issues. If you prefer to work with senior management, you might focus on strategy.

Any of these will support this client's change to a better future. Successful independent consultants target a level or kind of person as their ideal client.

When you choose the signals you want to address, you can craft your content marketing strategy to reach the people who see and hear those signals.

Choose the kinds of people with whom you want to work. For example, do you prefer to work with individuals or teams who do the work? Their managers? Their managers' managers? The nine consulting roles (see Figure 1.1: Possible Consulting Roles, p. 4), work at all levels of the organization.

Since one consultant cannot work with everyone up and down the organization, consider how you might Collaborate with Other Consultants (p. 213).

Alternatively, if you're discussing a potential engagement with a client, you might ask questions such as:

1. What challenges keep you up at night?
2. What do the people you work with or lead say about their challenges?

3. How satisfied or dissatisfied are the people with their work?

Remember to empathize with your clients. They want to do a good job, regardless of their role. If you can clarify the signals you address, they are more likely to hire you.

2.2 Clarify the Signals You Choose to Address

As you list the signals you see, choose where you want to support your client's changes for now. You might change your practice later, as you gain more experience. That's when you can choose to Adapt and Evolve Your Successful Practice (p. 245).

As you describe your list of signals, focus on the concrete details. Concrete details include the five senses, specifically, what people see, hear, and feel. Consider adding measurement to that, especially if some people in the organization appear to see—and then believe—things differently than others.

The statements in the previous section have concrete details. Based on those statements, here's the list I generated from the statements in the previous section:

- Are you trying to work on two or more projects at the same time and not finishing anything? (This question addresses the too many meetings and multitasking statements.)
- Are your estimates all wrong because you get interrupted all the time? (This question addresses the multitasking and the meeting problems.)
- Are you unable to collaborate with the rest of the team because all of you work separately? (This team-focused question addresses the lack of transparency and coordination, and the lack of finishing.)
- Would you like a trustworthy short-term prediction of how long the next bit of work might take? (This addresses the manager's need for estimates and the manager's lack of trust in those estimates.)

- Would you like to know why you can see people working, but they don't appear to have anything to show for it? (This is a management-focused question about the lack of finishing and the apparent squandering of time.)
- Would you like to understand how the team predicts its duration?

If you can see your client nodding and saying, "Yes, these are my problems!" you've generated actual pain points, the signals your ideal clients see.

Test the pain points *for yourself* by asking, "So what?" Or "Why does this matter?" after each pain point. The pain points are signals of deeper problems. When you ask "So what?" you learn more about those problems.

For example, the first bullet is:

- Are you trying to work on two or more projects at one time and not getting anything done?

If you ask, "So what?" or "Why does this matter?" after that, you might generate this list:

- People take a long time to finish work.
- We can't easily manage the project portfolio.
- We don't have time to plan for the next small chunk of work as a team because everyone's frantically trying to finish "their" work.

You can decide if you want to build products and services to address these pain points. For years, I focused on the team's approach in the face of multitasking requests. My ideal clients were project managers or project teams.

After I wrote several more books, I changed my focus to what various levels of management can do to stop multitasking. I changed my ideal clients to middle and senior management.

Sometimes, what we observe is not a signal or a pain point. Here's an example:

You don't have an agile culture.

That might or might not be accurate. However, it fails the empathy test with the potential client. What does an agile culture mean? Why is it valuable? Why is the lack of an agile culture a problem?

I gained a client because another consultant said these exact words to his potential client. That client came to me and said, "So, we don't have an agile culture. As an organization, we're still making money. What's the problem here?"

I asked them other questions to see what they wanted to achieve. They needed a culture of experimentation. As a byproduct, they did create *their* agile culture. But they chose to change because they now understood why.

Many statements like these do not matter to prospective clients. Instead, consider the various changes a client would need to achieve that culture. Here are some examples of signals and the so-what:

- It's too hard to change our decisions, so we continue on a questionable path.
- We don't release finished increments of products fast enough, so we don't learn what our customers think of or want from our product.
- We have to commit to features and plans very far in advance, so we can't take advantage of market changes.

Those "so" clauses might be the signals or the pain points.

Clients reinforce their culture—the way things are now—for any number of reasons. In my experience, they don't realize they have choices. That's why successful consultants build empathy with the client and create an effective client relationship.

Build Empathy with Clients' Problems

Make sure you don't fall into the trap of blaming the client for the way things are. Help clients see their problems, but not feel stupid, bad, or wrong.

Instead, help the client agree with your assessment of the pain points.

Test the empathy of your pain points with these questions:

- Would a potential client feel I'm faulting them for not doing something right?
- Would a potential client ask this question, "Why is this a problem?" or "So what?"

If your tests fail, rewrite the pain points so your potential client can agree. I like to think about the client nodding their head, saying, "Yes, this consultant understands what it's like for me to work here. Maybe this consultant can offer me other choices."

When you generate the pain points you have the expertise to solve, you help your ideal clients choose you. And, your not-ideal clients don't select you—a win-win.

Next, let's discuss how to define the problems you want to—and can—solve with your skills.

2.3 Define the Problems You Solve

Which problems do you want to help your clients solve?

Every potential client has plenty of problems—even those who think they have no problems.

You might think that clients who don't acknowledge their signals or problems are not ideal clients. But more often, these clients have systems that prevent them from seeing any signals at all, until it's very late. If you can help those clients see early warning signs, you can be even more valuable than you, or they, imagined.

We Have No Problems

Long ago, I had dinner with a potential client. They told me their projects were all on time, their customers were thrilled with them, and they were on track for hundreds of percent revenue growth in one year.

I congratulated them and asked these questions:

- How do you know your current approaches will still fit when you have to hire another couple of hundred people to continue to do all this work?

- How do you know you couldn't grow even more if you had a little support from me?"

Sometimes, clients need to learn to anticipate their problems and ask for your help in advance, and you can help them do that.

2.4 See the System that Creates These Pains

Sometimes, when I teach the idea of pain points to consultants, they say, "The client doesn't use X model," "Y framework," or "Z tool." See Appendix B: Consider These Consulting Tools (p. 257) for more information.

Our models, frameworks, and tools help us see the client's system. And, if we only think in terms of these models, frameworks, or tools, we create blind spots. Instead, consider the system that causes the client's pain.

Your clients will tell you they are unique, and they are. Successful independent consultants can use many possible frames to see their clients' realities. Avoid feeling as if you're bound to one way of thinking.

"I Had to Remove Blinders to Serve the Client"

"I used to be a one-agile-framework-rules-them-all consultant. I thought that framework worked everywhere—maybe with tweaks, but it always worked. I never considered that some people couldn't use that framework.

One client taught me differently. In the next workshop, I had two representative teams. One team could use the framework successfully. Turns out that team represented just 10% of the company's revenue. The other team, which represented 90% of the revenue, could not use this approach. I needed to find other solutions and fast.

"I read all I could about the other frameworks. They weren't really right by themselves, either.

"I'd built trust with the client. I'd chosen to co-create their approach with them. We used the principles I knew that had served them well up until now. We created a system that worked for more groups.

"I hadn't fully seen their system before I started to teach. Before I taught this client, I knew my framework was the One Right Way. I feel as if I removed blinders.

—An experienced agile consultant.

You can work with specific models, frameworks, and tools. However, sometimes, those "standard" solutions can trap you into commodity work as a consultant or a contractor.

Remember, clients pay you for changes and results.

Use everything—models, frameworks, tools—to serve your clients. Watch that your various tools don't create blinders that prevent you from empathizing with your clients. The more flexible you are with your thinking, the more you empathize with your clients about their current state.

2.5 **Choose Your Ideal Clients**

Once you realize which problems you can solve, you can decide which kinds of people you want as clients. Consider this approach:

1. The type of industry. For example, I'm an expert in managing high-tech product development. That includes IT and Engineering organizations—but not construction. Construction projects and companies *use* high-tech products, but they don't *develop* high-tech products.
2. The function. Many independent consultants focus on one function in the organization, such as product management, HR, Sales, and more.
3. The level at which you want to work. Some consultants focus on individuals or teams, the lowest hierarchical level in the company, and that target market is extensive. Other consultants focus on senior management in Fortune 25 companies, and that market is more limited.

Once you know the kinds of people you want as ideal clients, you can decide which problems you want to solve and how. Refer to Figure 1.1: Possible Consulting Roles (p. 4) to see which roles feel best in different situations.

And once you know your ideal clients, you can decide which content marketing to use to attract which people.

2.6 **Update Your Skills and Preferences**

And, as you gain more experience, recognize when you learn more. Consider the ideas in Assess Previous Work (p. 11) to determine where you are growing and which signals you want to address now. That assessment will help you decide which potential clients to choose.

2.7 **Now Try This to Identify Your Ideal Clients**

Which problems can you solve with your various skills and perspectives? That's your potential market. You can identify and clarify your potential market when you match your skills to the changes your clients need *and* will pay for.

Independent consultants can use a small potential market of clients. However, they do need a large enough market to offer various services based on the consultant's skills.

1. Generate a list of five to ten signals clients see that you have the skills to address.
2. For each signal, answer the "So what" or "Why this matters" to those clients. Clarify which of your skills you can apply to those signals.
3. Brainstorm a list of ten to twenty ideal clients who need you to solve these problems. Consider all these options for that potential client list: company names, company titles, or industries. If you have fewer than ten possible clients, see if you are artificially restricting the kind of work you want to do.

Now that you've clarified how to match your skills with a client market, consider how you will help those potential clients know who you are and what you offer.

CHAPTER 3

Attract Clients With Content Marketing

Now that you know which problems you want to help your clients solve, it's time to attract those ideal clients.

There's an easy way for people to know who you are: content marketing. That's writing and speaking about your specific skills and the pain points you choose to address for clients. Content marketing helps you and others understand your value and skills—and your ideal clients.

3.1 Why Content Marketing?

It works.

Howard Shenson, in *The Complete Guide to Consulting Success*, SHE97, wrote that the consultants who spoke grossed over $100,000, and the consultants who didn't only grossed $30,000 or less. (In the third edition, he noted that consultants who spoke and wrote grossed substantially more than their consulting colleagues who did not write and speak.)

Some people call this "thought leadership." I prefer to call it thought-provoking.

Whatever you call it, know that the more you create and publicize the content that speaks to your preferred clients, the more your ideal clients will find you.

What if you think you hate speaking and writing as forms of content marketing? Consider trying it before you decide it's not for you. That's because content marketing works in many ways:

1. You never have to use traditional promotion: to advertise or use someone else to sell your services.
2. Other people share your content. Those soft referrals help other people refer to you as an expert.
3. You build trust with potential clients. They will ask for you *by name* because your content already proved your worth to them.

As a side benefit, the more consultants create content, the more they reinforce their learning and expertise. In effect, the more you speak and write, the more you realize what works and what doesn't.

When I meet consultants who think marketing is slimy or icky, those consultants often confuse content marketing with other kinds of marketing or with selling.

Let's set the record straight. Peter Drucker in *Management: Tasks, Responsibilities, Practices*, DRU73 said:

"... the aim of marketing is to make selling superfluous. The aim of marketing is to know and understand the customer so well that the product or service fits him and sells itself."

I don't want to do anything that smacks of selling, advertising, or promotion. However, I attract people to my products and services via content marketing. Some of those people sell themselves on my products and services.

Think of marketing as free education for your potential clients. When you explain your expertise so they understand, your readers or viewers will see what you have to offer.

Don't worry about this idea of "free" education. If the client has the need, your content—even if you offer step-by-step instructions—is not enough for the client to act. That's why successful consultants select which role to use with each client, as in Figure 1.1: Possible Consulting Roles (p. 4).

If you have not yet thought about content marketing, consider reading *This Is Marketing: You Can't Be Seen Until You Learn to See*, GOD18.

3.2 Frame Your Successful Content Marketing Strategy

Content marketing consists of:

- Relevant and valuable content that you create based on your unique expertise,
- That you deliver regularly,
- Where that content attracts and retains clients.

For example, an email newsletter, free videos, or blog posts are all content marketing.

You might change which content you deliver as you change your business model. Or how. As you create content, you might discover that you can broaden or narrow your definition of ideal clients.

However, the strategy is to create unique content that you deliver regularly. That delivery helps you to attract and retain clients.

The more you think about how your marketing tactics fulfill your marketing strategy, the more likely you will attract your ideal clients.

While your content marketing *strategy* might stay consistent (writing and speaking), your marketing *tactics* will almost certainly change. As long as your potential clients can discover you with your content marketing, you're probably doing enough of the right things.

Consider how you can drip content regularly to attract and retain potential clients.

3.3 Drip Your Content Marketing

Many marketing and sales books discuss a "funnel" where potential clients enter the top. Assuming they are an ideal client, the client buys one or more of your products or services. You both profit—they gain the benefits of your services, and you receive payment.

Then, at some point, the client "exits" the funnel.

However, I don't like the idea of my ideal clients exiting my funnel. I want to retain them—as long as they remain my ideal clients. The more you regularly release content, the longer you can retain current and potential clients in your content marketing ecosystem.

Not every potential client wants to hear from you the same way. That's why you might consider a periodic newsletter with some content and a blog for different content. You might create conference talks from any of that content—or create a talk first and then write several posts or newsletters.

If you prefer making videos, substitute the word video for any of the above.

Why Email Newsletters Work

For years, people have predicted the "death" of email. However, email newsletters won't die for the foreseeable future.

That's because email is permission-based marketing. When someone subscribes to your email newsletter, they chose to receive your content. They acted and gave you permission to contact them.

At this point, there is no other marketing venue that encourages permission-based marketing. No social media site shows your content to all the people who follow or like you. Those sites use algorithms to decide who to show your content to.

Email marketing is your place to attract clients to your work. You own it. You choose how to use it.

Successful consultants find a way to create and deliver content to their potential clients on a regular basis. The more regular you are, the more you build trust with these potential clients. Some of these potential clients turn into ideal clients—and might even persuade themselves to buy from you.

That's because as you drip your content, potential clients understand why you do what you do. That's your brand.

3.4 Content Marketing Defines Your Brand

In the previous chapter, you considered the problems you can solve and for whom. I didn't ask you to write down your "why," why you do the work. The more you build content, the easier it is for potential clients to see why you do this work.

You don't have to see it. Your readers and listeners will.

Content marketing creates a reinforcing feedback loop with these benefits:

- Attraction: Potential clients become aware of you because of something you wrote or said. If you invite people to subscribe to your newsletter, you gain their permission to send them more useful content.
- Build relationships: The more you write and speak, the more you create and reinforce a trusting relationship with these people. Some of them will become clients.
- Expansion: Add more content with the questions and comments people have from your writing and speaking. While you might start with a narrow context for those questions and comments, other consumers of your content probably have similar concerns. This additional content helps you attract other potential clients.
- Referrals: If your content is good enough, some people—even if they aren't clients—will refer others to your work. Your content marketing helps other people attract more people to your content.

Everyone will create their strategies and tactics for their drip content marketing. Let's start with creating a strategy for content marketing.

3.5 Create a Positive Content Marketing Feedback Loop

If you've ever heard feedback from a microphone screeching, you've experienced a feedback loop. The initial sound feeds back into the microphone, enhancing the sound until someone (thankfully) turns off the microphone or the speakers. That's a tight positive feedback loop.

Positive feedback loops help us amplify and reinforce the value of our original work. Conversely, negative feedback loops decrease or dampen the original. If you stop creating more content, that dampens your feedback loop.

I use writing, speaking, and referrals as my initial content. Here's how all three create a reinforcing feedback loop:

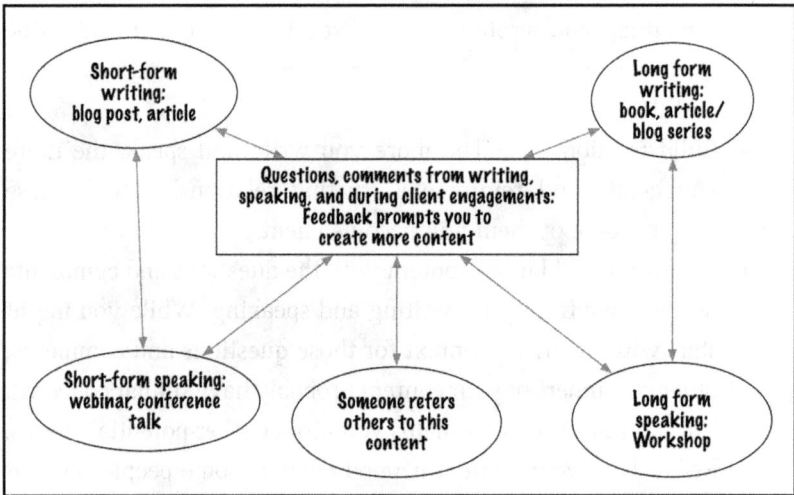

Figure 3.1: Interplay Between Writing and Speaking

Imagine you've given a talk at a conference. Several people ask you questions about your content afterward. You take notes and create several more email newsletters, blog posts, or videos based on their questions. Or, you create an article for publication elsewhere.

The same dynamic occurs when you deliver a client engagement. As people at the client ask you questions or comment on ideas, you can use those questions and comments to generate more content for your marketing. (Always anonymize the client when you speak or write about their challenges. Even though each client is unique, their challenges and problems tend to be universal.)

Writing and speaking reinforce each other and help consultants create more content. The more content you create, the more likely other people will forward your content to their colleagues.

Eventually, you might want to collect some of your content into a series of articles, books, or workshops.

Because this is a reinforcing feedback loop, consultants can learn as they write and speak. That learning can help you understand more about the value you offer to potential clients.

Here are all the positive feedback loops that I use as strategies:

- The more I write and speak, the more potential clients hear my message. I have an opportunity to invite more people to my drip content marketing.
- The more people ask me questions, the more content I can create. The more content, the more people come to my talks and read on my site.
- The more I answer questions, the more I learn. Based on what I learned, I create more content.

I want people to remove themselves from my email list when my content no longer works for them. They are no longer my ideal clients.

Successful independent consultants don't need a huge number of people on their email lists, or social media followers. Instead, when consultants ask for permission and use attraction marketing, they often find the right clients.

Consider these strategies for your continual content marketing:

- Speak to and with relevant audiences.
- Write about what interests you, as long as it's relevant to your potential clients.
- Encourage people to share your content.

Now, consider your content marketing tactics.

3.6 Define Your Content Marketing Tactics

Your content marketing helps potential clients learn that you exist and the kinds of problems you solve. Not *how* you solve problems, but *which* issues you address with your expertise.

Each successful consultant selects their tactics. The three major tactics are writing, speaking, and asking for referrals. What's the "right" mix for you? (If you're looking for networking opportunities, see Build Presence with Active Marketing. p. 53.)

Your content marketing tactics reflect your preferences:

- Do you prefer writing to public speaking? Write and publish broadly to invite people back to your site to sign up for your email newsletter. Add some speaking to your content marketing, and your potential clients will discover you.
- You can reach potential clients as a speaker, especially if you are an extrovert. Select conferences and venues that attract your ideal clients.
- Ask people to share your content with others who will find it relevant and helpful.
- And, once you complete an engagement, ask for a referral to other people who might share this client's challenges.

You may have to experiment to get the "right" mix of content marketing for your business.

While I love my public speaking, my writing appears to attract more of my ideal clients. And I can control what and when I write, which is why that's first on my tactics.

3.6.1 *Write to Share Your Unique Expertise*

Consider all of these writing outlets to showcase your expertise:

1. Write and send your newsletter to your subscribers. Then, publish it on your site and create an archive so new readers can see if they want to subscribe.

2. Write posts and articles on your blog/site.

3. Write articles for someone else's site—with any luck, for pay. And see if you can republish that work on your site after some time, say thirty or sixty days after the site publishes your article.

If you have the time and interest, also consider writing and publishing a book. However, books take time to write. And books in progress offer no value to you or to your clients yet. If you do decide to write a book, make sure you have a professional cover and layout.

Consider "Publishers" or Aggregators for Short Pieces

As of this writing, LinkedIn and Medium offer ways for you to publish your writing. They want to attract readers to their sites, not attract readers to you.

I recommend you always publish on your site first, and then republish on other sites. Both LinkedIn and Medium do *not* attract your ideal readers. Instead, they offer *some* of their ideal readers access to your material.

Because they are social media, their algorithms will choose who sees your posts. Consider how you want to use aggregators or publishers. I'll discuss more about social media later in this chapter.

Your blog has two kinds of reach: the people who follow your blog and want to read what you write. Those people are part of your attraction content marketing.

The second audience is the people who find your content through search. There are plenty of "experts" who will tell you to stuff search terms or links in your site so you can rank higher in searches. That feels slimy to me. Instead, I recommend you write consistently about topics that will attract the clients you want to serve.

Consider writing articles or short pieces for other sites, too. Those sites will introduce you to their audience. Over the years, I've established long-term relationships with several websites. I often take a contrarian position—based on my experience—which allows me to offer different and unique content. That position cements my expertise with people who might be my ideal clients.

Not everyone who reads your work is a potential client. That doesn't matter to me—if I write content that showcases my expertise, my readers will either introduce my work to potential clients or ask me questions that prompt more content. I don't have to reach the real buyer right away—I can reach other people who can introduce me to the person who can buy.

The more I write, the more I learn what I know and how to express that knowledge.

I also like to speak.

3.6.2 *Speak to Establish Your Expertise*

I use many in-person and remote speaking alternatives to showcase my expertise:

1. Speak at a meetup or professional group.
2. Speak at a "small," primarily regional conference.
3. Speak at a more extensive, international conference. One of the (few) benefits of the pandemic is that I could speak internationally without getting on a plane. I didn't have to travel to a large conference and then take advantage of my presence to speak at a local meetup.
4. Webinars, other people's, and yours.
5. Podcasts, other people's, and yours.
6. Speak and record videos for your video channel.

Speaking in person or remotely in real-time has its discovery benefits:

- Meetup and conference speaking help me learn what's happening in different locales. More people become aware of my work, and

I invite them to my newsletter. Local meetups and conferences offer the benefit of introducing you to people in your desired location. Not all meetups and conferences offer the same value. Decide what value you might receive from these opportunities.

- When I speak at other people's webinars, I leverage their marketing.
- Podcast interviews help me introduce my work to another audience. Use podcasting to practice specific ideas, learn from others, and have a great conversation with a host.
- Your podcast allows you to create or leverage your content. Every podcast requires time to build an audience. However, the more you podcast, the faster you build your audience. In my experience, your own podcast requires a lot of investment of your time so you can build enough content.

Video recordings don't offer you real-time interaction, but might offer you a way to test new ideas and create content marketing of your older ideas. (Don't worry about videos for your "old" content. Your old content is new to people who have not yet seen it. Older ideas don't age like stinky cheese—useful ideas maintain their freshness.)

Not all events offer significant attendee interaction. That's why I create an invitation on my last slide for people to subscribe to my newsletter and connect with me on LinkedIn.

Decide about the kind of in-person speaking you want to perform. (Yes, speaking is part performance and part content.)

If you speak for a webinar organizer, verify these potential problems in advance. Will the organizer:

- Compensate you for speaking?
- Record your talk?
- Give you that recording?
- Put your content behind a paywall after you speak?

Choose your speaking fee depending on the answers to these questions.

For example, I have this guideline: I expect payment if the organizer makes money from my talk. In addition, some organizers create libraries of experts' talks. I expect a royalty share if the organizer continues to make money from my talk.

I do not have a podcast and do not plan to start one. Creating a podcast and continuing it takes more time than I want. It might be the right kind of content creation option for you—especially if you don't like to write. I love to speak on other people's podcasts.

As I write this, I'm experimenting with videos on my YouTube channel. My experiment is new, so I have no data yet to share.

Remember this about speaking: when consultants speak, they initiate relationships with the people in the room or watching. Start with empathy.

However you start to create IP (Intellectual Property), you can repurpose it.

3.6.3 Repurpose Your IP

Once you've started to write and speak, you can repurpose your IP.

You might write a series of blog posts that become one talk. Or, you give a talk and realize you want to write more about these topics.

If you write a book, you can write blog posts that are tangential to the topics in the book that invite your readers to buy the book. And, you can give talks that offer deep insight into one or two of the topics, to invite people to read the book.

Once you have IP in one form, you can adapt it into another. That's the whole point of Figure 3.1: Interplay Between Writing and Speaking (p. 32).

And you can use social media to reinforce your IP.

3.6.4 Use Social Media to Reinforce Your Message

Some of my consulting colleagues appear (to me) to spend a lot of time on their chosen social media. They tend to post one to three sentences of content many times during the day.

These colleagues tell me their social media activity helps them connect with potential clients. That's terrific. If your potential clients use social media, yes, share content on any platform that fits your values and needs.

However, while you might use social media as content marketing, it is not permission-based. The various sites decide who will see your content. You don't get to decide. That's why I write on my site first, and then republish to the various platforms. That often means the media companies decide my content does not deserve to be shown to my followers. I can live with that.

I recommend these guidelines:

- Learn the culture of the platform. What is acceptable to discuss? How do people treat each other? Does that fit with your messages?
- Be consistent in your use of the platform. Post content that helps people become aware of your expertise.
- Decide if you will share—or not—any content that does not relate to unique expertise. For example, I recommend you avoid social commentary—although that appears to work for many of my colleagues.

Because social media seems pervasive in many of our lives, your ideal clients might not see your messages because the channels are quite noisy. Most people with the power to buy my services do not use Twitter, although some use LinkedIn.

However, I use social media to reinforce my messages. I inform social media when I:

- Publish a newsletter or a blog post.
- Read someone else's content that I think my followers would enjoy.
- Appear on a podcast or in a video.

You probably have many other great ideas for how to use social media.

I recommend this guideline: Make sure you have a newsletter sign-up box on every page of your site. Then, when you post a link on any social media channel, that link will offer a signup to your newsletter.

Let social media reinforce your messages back on your site. You might even build some relationships on the platforms.

If you try to connect with people on a social media site *first*, that's active marketing, not content marketing.

3.7 Network with Your Professional Community

So far, I've suggested specific ways to create and use your specific content. Because you create content, networking at professional meetings can be a part of your content marketing.

When I talk about networking, I mean to build relationships before you "need" them. While you might offer your business card to everyone in the room, avoid forcing your card on everyone.

Instead, focus on how you can get to know people who *might* be interested in what you have to offer as a consultant. In my experience, a person's title has little to do with their ability to hire a consultant. (See Build the Client Relationship, p. 71, for more details about how some of my clients have found and hired me.)

That means you can network with your colleagues as part of your content marketing. As an independent consultant, you can focus on the relationship side of networking, not to force your business card on everyone in the room.

That's a slow-build approach to creating your professional network. Start with how people perceive you.

3.7.1 *How Do Others Perceive You?*

I'm short and female, which means most people don't perceive me as a threat to their knowledge or position. I happily share my opinions about anything, but since I work to stay empathetic, very few people take a dislike to me immediately.

However, some people seem to be born irritators.

At a speaker dinner several years ago, I sat across the table from a fellow speaker. He pontificated, gestured, and tried to set himself up as an all-around expert on almost everything. I ignored him as much as possible. Then, he quoted a line from one of my books.

I asked him where he'd written that. Maybe I had unknowingly quoted him.

He said, "No, I didn't write that. I subscribe to this woman's newsletter—" and that's when he looked at my name badge.

I smiled and decided I was fine with him quoting me.

I could have reacted differently—and I was all set to do so. Then I realized the world was big enough for him to quote me and maybe even use my work in his practice. Would I benefit? Maybe. And it didn't matter if I benefited directly or not. I produce content for other people to use. He's using it.

I'm not worried about being intimidating or threatening. I am worried about looking like a jerk. Ask yourself, and maybe a few trusted colleagues to tell you how others perceive you.

The more human, we as consultants are, the more likely we are to find enough clients because we start the client relationship from the time someone sees us. No one will refer you if they're not comfortable with you.

Once you have an idea about how others might react to you, consider ways you can network when speaking.

3.7.2 *Network When Speaking*

When I speak in person, I make a point of networking with the people in the room. Because I want to focus on how people react to my content, I prepare the room as early as possible. As I check the presentation, I ask people in the room if the slides look straight on the screen. I also ask the people in the back if my microphone has a good sound level.

If I plan to have some activities in the presentation, I enlist the help of the people who are already in the room. These little requests for help predispose the audience to like me, the speaker.

Then, assuming I have more time, I walk around the first few rows or tables, introducing myself. I ask people to explain their role and where they work. If possible, I use some of those people as examples in my presentation.

These small actions show I focus on the audience, and their challenges and concerns.

Even if conferences made the print on badges larger, I would still walk around, shake hands and ask for a verbal introduction. That helps me create a small connection with people.

If you're speaking remotely, you can adapt these ideas to say hello before you start your presentation. I like to ask how many people are in which role, and other demographic questions.

Networking while you speak is just one way to network. You can also network as a volunteer.

3.7.3 *Network As a Volunteer*

For years, I volunteered for a local professional group, Boston SPIN (Software Process Improvement Network). I had the opportunity to meet about a hundred local people every month for a decade. I was the Program Chair for most of that time, which meant I found and introduced the speaker at the monthly meeting.

I chose SPIN because those people were more likely to know they needed someone like me. And because I introduced the speaker each month, I networked inside and outside the community to find new speakers and to build relationships.

I've volunteered for the Agile Alliance conferences for many years as a track chair, track reviewer, and experience report shepherd. That volunteering introduced me to other consultants. In addition, I inadvertently discovered clients.

I didn't volunteer for those conferences to find clients. Instead, I offered my time and received more than I expected in return.

I've also contributed to bodies of knowledge as part of "giving back" to the community. I was the Co-Chair for the first edition of the Agile Practice Guide. I contributed to some of the learning objectives for the ICAgile bodies of knowledge. I consider this work part of my professional "dues"—where I use my expertise and try to enrich the community.

These activities have helped me meet more colleagues and, sometimes, clients. I happen to like being part of the community.

3.7.4 *Ask for a Referral After Starting a Relationship*

Once you have a professional community, decide when to ask for testimonials and referrals.

Early in my consulting career, I sometimes asked people for testimonials about my volunteer work because I performed project and risk management. My volunteer work was relevant to my consulting.

However, decide when you want to ask for a referral in a networking relationship. Start with this question, "Do you know of someone who could use my kind of services?"

Even clients sometimes say, "No." Then, a week later, I receive an email from someone they referred to me.

I will take every opportunity to build relationships with people both in-person and online.

Consistent content marketing works for me.

3.8 **Create Consistent Content**

I don't know how often I need to "touch" a person before they buy from me. Sometimes, my ideal client reads one article, and sometimes, the client has read my newsletter for ten years or longer. I only know this: the more I build awareness of my expertise, the more clients I have.

You might wonder about how to measure the effectiveness of your content marketing. I have only one measure: the number of people I attract to sign up for my newsletter. That's because content marketing is a long-term strategy. Newsletter subscribers are a better indication of my general marketing health than any other number.

In *Secrets of Consulting* WCO14, Weinberg says that consultants live in one of two states: too much work and not enough work. Drip content marketing aids you in solving that problem.

I've been in both states, and I prefer to manage the problem of too much work.

Here are some ideas to build your consistency:

- Choose a cadence of newsletter writing. I choose monthly because I also blog and write articles each week. If you don't write elsewhere, consider a weekly newsletter.
- If you can, choose a specific day of the month or week so your readers can depend on you.
- Decide on a speaking cadence. Can you speak at least once a month? If so, propose a talk to twelve meetups or conferences a year. While conferences offer specific submission windows, meetups always need speakers.
- Decide how you will network, both in person and online.

I choose the marketing activities that work for me. You are different, so you'll select your mix of marketing activities.

Decide on your strategy. Then, create tactics for your content marketing. Write down your marketing plan, so you don't forget anything.

3.9 Create Your Marketing Plan

Every consultant I meet has this problem: when to perform which activities for marketing. That's why I recommend you create your marketing plan.

You might have seen marketing plans that discuss social media. Most of those plans are called marketing calendars. This plan doesn't.

Instead, this plan focuses on building your IP (intellectual property), bit by bit.

Here are the pieces of the plan:

1. When do you want people to think of *you*?
2. Which people do you want to think of you? (Those people might be the person who can sign a purchase order. Or, it might be someone else, who can refer you to that person.
3. How will you help those people become aware of you? (Include writing, speaking, referrals, and networking.)

I update my marketing plan each year every time I change my mix of products and services. I also write a new marketing plan every January, for the new year.

Review the ideas earlier in this chapter in Content Marketing Defines Your Brand (p. 31) to see how you can use permission and attraction-based content marketing to help potential clients become aware of you and your work.

As you write your marketing plan, ask yourself which activities will help your potential clients become *aware* of your unique expertise. Which activities allow you to *invite* people to your newsletter or other writing so they realize you can help them with their challenges? Which other activities might prompt non-ideal clients to refer you to others?

Those tactics will help you create your marketing plan.

I have seen marketing plans that look like outlines, roadmaps, and systems diagrams. Allan Dib, in his excellent *The 1-Page Marketing Plan: Get New Customers, Make More Money, And Stand Out From The Crowd* DIB16, offers a canvas.

I happen to use an outline-oriented plan. Don't overthink the format of your marketing plan. Write it down and then iterate on it.

3.10 Consider This Marketing Plan Template

This outline works for me. Try it and see if it works for you, too.

1. Title of the plan: Marketing Plan for "your business name," for a given year.
2. This prompt clarifies your work: "I want people to think of me when they have these problems." List those problems.
3. This prompt clarifies your ideal clients: "I want these kinds of people to think of me." List your ideal clients, economic, technical, and coach buyers.
4. These people can find me in these ways: and then create separate lists for all of your activities: writing, speaking, videos, referrals, and networking.

I recommend you have a *minimum* of three bullets in each of these lists. The more you push yourself to generate more items in each list, the more resilient your business model will be.

For example, I want people to think of me when they plan their work, both for the project portfolio and product roadmaps. The problems I want to address include planning for a too-long duration; requiring estimates from others; and wanting a specific date for delivery.

Here are the ideal clients for that work: middle managers in smaller organizations; the project portfolio or operations team; and product leaders. The technical or coach buyers are people who feel the pain of the middle or senior leadership wanting all those things.

The coach or technical buyers will find me through my blog and newsletter. The economic buyers will find me through webinar partnerships with several organizations.

Notice that last sentence. When I wrote down my list, I realized I need more ways to find economic buyers. That's the point of the yearly marketing plan.

Test the marketing plan template to see if you are trying to be everything to everyone—or if you are taking a too-narrow approach to your business. Here's how I test the plan:

- If I address too many problems, I might look like a commodity. My clients won't understand the unique value I offer.

- If I address too few problems, I might look as if I don't have enough breadth to do an excellent job as a consultant.
- If I can't think of enough ideal clients, I might not have a viable business model.
- If I can't think of how to create intellectual property in many ways so people can find me, I might not have a viable business model.

Your marketing plan helps you verify your business model.

3.11 Consider These Content Marketing Tips

As you work on your content marketing, review your actions to use these tips.

- Integrate your marketing with your consulting.
- Create consistent content.
- Keep your content on your site, your online home.

Let's start with integrating your content development with your consulting activities.

3.11.1 Tip: Integrate Your Marketing With Your Consulting

When I say to integrate your marketing with your consulting, I mean to write and speak about the ideas you bring to your consulting. And to consult about what you write and speak about.

Consider content marketing: relevant and valuable writing and speaking so your ideal clients will choose you. When you integrate your marketing with your consulting, you might see how to develop *more* products and services that reflect that content.

When I meet consultants who separate their marketing from their consulting, they often tell me they're concerned their writing or speaking isn't "good enough." Or that they'll look foolish or wrong. These are too-typical traps for writers. See the book *Free Your Inner Nonfiction Writer: Educate, Influence, and Entertain Your Readers* ROT22 for details on these and other traps and what to do instead.

Apply your consulting skills to that problem. What would you recommend a client do in this case? Here are some ideas, based on the consulting grid in Figure 1.1: Possible Consulting Roles (p. 4):

- Do you need a teacher? Take writing or speaking workshops. Just as you recommend training to your clients, consider learning from experts. I recommend you take workshops from people who have significant experience writing and speaking. Look at their body of work and see if their work resonates with you. Yes, I suggest you use their content marketing to see if they are the right teacher for you.
- Maybe you need a reflective observer or a counselor? Arrange for feedback for your speaking. When I practice a talk, I record it in advance. Then I play it back and watch: did I say what I wanted to say? That's a form of feedback. You might ask someone to offer you feedback after you record a talk or deliver it. For years, I also recorded my talks so I could assess my content and performance.
- Do you need a coach or partner? You might want to work with a fellow writer or speaker to see how they work.

The best way to improve any skills, especially writing and speaking, is consistent practice. And use the ideas in Define Your Unique Value (p. 3) to manage any Imposter Syndrome you have.

The more often you write and speak, the more you integrate your marketing with your consulting. You reinforce your unique value to both you and your potential clients.

Consistency helps you recognize your value and create more content.

3.11.2 *Tip: Consistency Matters*

I can't guarantee that your ideal clients will find you if you create consistent content. However, I know that if you *don't* create content, those people won't find you.

I recommend you publish something, as in writing or speaking, at least three times a week. If you're starting a business from scratch, see the ideas in Plan for Three Months of Active Marketing (p. 66).

I use calendar reminders to create and publish newsletters and blog posts. Those reminders help me stay consistent.

In addition, because I integrate my marketing with my consulting, I reinforce my offerings in the eyes of my ideal clients.

The more content you create, the more you might wonder where to put it all. That's why I recommend you put everything on your online home first. Then, if you want, republish somewhere else.

3.11.3 *Tip: Maintain Your Content on Your Site*

As you write and speak, you realize you have content in various forms:

- Blog posts
- Newsletters
- Articles
- Videos
- Podcasts

And maybe more. What do you do with all that content?

Let's start with your writing. I strongly recommend you post all your writing on *your* site, on the relevant pages. Make a newsletter archive page and possibly an articles page.

Create a newsletter archive, preferably on your site, not your newsletter provider. Remember, your newsletter provider does *not* market you—the provider markets its services.

Republish your content on social media *after* publishing it on your site.

Various social media sites offer you ways to increase your potential audience. Always publish on your site first. Then, post that content to social media, with a link back to your site.

When you add specific archive pages, such as for your newsletter and articles, you show the breadth and depth of your unique expertise. And since you have a newsletter signup form on each page, you can take advantage of a reader joining your newsletter.

Creating writing archives is relatively easy. I don't recommend you place the actual videos and podcasts on your site at this time because you'll have to pay too much for bandwidth. Instead, use a hosting service and link to that content.

However, use the same idea as your newsletter—maintain an archive page with links to the videos and podcasts.

Your potential clients will still see the breadth of your content, just from listing the episode titles.

3.12 Now Try This to Help Clients Discover You With Content Marketing

Start your content marketing as soon as you think you might want to be a consultant. Content marketing offers you two distinct benefits: you'll learn what you think as you write and speak. And you can start making a name for yourself before you need it. The earlier you start your content marketing, the less pressure you might feel as you build your consulting business.

I said that content marketing consists of:

- Relevant and valuable content that you create based on your unique expertise,
- That you deliver regularly,
- Where that content attracts and retains potential clients.

In your consulting notebook:

Make a list of at least twelve topics you can use for speaking and writing. This content is what you want to share, based on your unique expertise. You can use these topics for your newsletter, blog posts, articles, and speaking. (Consider using the idea bank and fieldstones as in *Free Your Inner Nonfiction Writer* ROT22.)

Make a list of the writing platforms, such as your blog, your newsletter, and other sites you will use. How often will you write in each of these places?

Generate a list of speaking possibilities that you want. I recommend you choose a combination of conferences, podcasts, and meetings. Make a list of twelve places you could speak this year.

However, content marketing takes time. If you want clients *now*, add active marketing to your marketing mix.

CHAPTER 4

Build Presence with Active Marketing

In content marketing, your IP speaks for you. As long as you create more and more IP, your ideal clients will find you.

However, you might be in the same position I was when I started my business. I had not written articles or spoken about my expertise before I started my consulting practice.

While content marketing is passive in the sense that you continue to publish your content and people find you, active marketing requires outreach. You speak for yourself.

In the Introduction, I explained that I had three weeks of notice for my layoff when I decided to start consulting. During those three weeks, I called everyone I knew and networked, explaining I was starting a new venture as a consultant.

In addition, I networked with some of the local professional groups and landed two speaking engagements. I called several local professional groups to see when they had opportunities for me to speak. Luckily, two of them did have dates for me to speak that fall, and I delivered two presentations.

I also volunteered at a third professional group. That volunteering allowed me to network with more people every month.

I spent September, October, and November using the active marketing techniques in this chapter. I built enough presence to start my business.

By the start of December, I had:

- Delivered two talks at local meetups.
- Written one article.
- Sold one workshop to one client.

While I did not make enough money that year to replace my salary, I had a good start on a sustainable business.

I listened to the questions people had from my talks and the workshop. Because I learned from those experiences, I wrote more content and spoke more, generating more content marketing. The following year, with content marketing alone, I earned more than enough to replace my salary.

Active marketing will help you create your presence, regardless of your location.

While I prefer content marketing, active marketing works if you need clients.

Here's how active marketing works:

You invite a person to a conversation. Hopefully, you know that person already. Or someone in a previous discussion introduced the two of you.

You explain a little about what you do in that conversation, focusing on your value because that's what sets you apart from everyone else. During the conversation, offer some value to the person, such as mentioning something you read that reminds you of their situation. Finally, ask them to keep you in mind if they or someone in their network needs what you do.

However, you need to finish some prerequisites before you have that conversation:

- A robust online profile.
- A professional email address.
- A bio for talks you will propose.
- A picture (headshot) you can use online.
- A phone number you can use for your business calls.
- A "script" so you know what to say for your active marketing.

You don't need a website yet, but you will in the future.

Active marketing still requires you to articulate your unique expertise and what success means to you, so make sure you finish all the activities in Define Your Unique Value (p. 3).

If you still need to build your network, start now. Even as you develop your online profile, start asking people to network with you.

4.1 Network with People

I'm using LinkedIn here because it's currently the gorilla of business networking.

With any luck, you've already added these people to your network.

- Current and previous colleagues.
- If you've met them, relatives, such as children of those colleagues.
- People you've met at meetups, conferences, and other professional groups.

Start now and add these folks to your network. As you network with them, remind people of where you met them.

In addition, if you've been working long enough that your friends' children now work, add those children, too. That's because they are a loose connection. Loose connections are the friends-of-friends or colleagues-of-colleagues.

Loose connections work well for networking because your networks are less likely to overlap. And that loose connection does not have an emotional investment in your success. Pfeffer has a great discussion on loose connections in *Power: Why Some People Have It and Others Don't* PFE10.

When you invite people to connect, they will review any of your online profiles, so create a robust profile.

4.2 Create a Robust Online Profile

When I started my business, we didn't have LinkedIn or websites. However, I did have a resume and (paper!) brochures.

Consultants need a robust online profile so people can find you wherever they might look:

- On LinkedIn (at this writing, which might change). As LinkedIn attracts competitors, consider where you want your profile to appear.
- Your resume.
- On your website.
- On any other online location, such as an about.me page.

Consider all these places. However, for business networking, I recommend you use LinkedIn. Your potential clients expect you to be there. In addition, LinkedIn has excellent guidance for your profile.

Do I Need to "Be Out There?"

A colleague who specializes in security told me he was considering consulting. He chose not to use social media. However, he had no experience and no picture on his LinkedIn profile. He didn't network in person or online. He didn't write or speak.

I asked him why his LinkedIn profile was so bare. He told me he specialized in security. I showed him half a dozen other consultants with a business similar to what he wanted.

He was too aware of security problems when telling people about himself. But he could not attract clients.

If you want clients to come to you as an independent consultant, find ways to market yourself online and in person.

A great profile has these parts in reading order:

1. A headline that describes your unique value or expertise.
2. A one-paragraph biography, or an "About" section, that people can read quickly.
3. A brief description of what you offer. Limit this section to between 150-250 words. Include some of the benefits people might see when working with you.

4. A list of your work experiences in reverse chronological order.

5. Any publications or awards.

Just because you read in order does not mean you have to write in the same order. You might start with your work experiences, mining those experiences to write your headline or bio. However, I'll describe these in reading order.

People read the headline first.

4.2.1 *Write a Brief Headline*

A headline helps people realize what you have to offer. If you are ready to say you're a consultant, do so. Do you want to add "speaker," "author," "facilitator," or some other description of your offerings? If so, add them.

Think of a headline about five to eight words long—just long enough to intrigue the reader. Otherwise, people will skip it. I recommend you leave all degrees off your headline.

For example, in my field, many people claim they are agile coaches. I searched LinkedIn and discovered 93,000 results for the term "agile coach." Even team or executive agile coach returned over 70,000 results each. So "agile coach" is not a sufficient headline.

Instead, consider how you might differentiate your unique skills using the value you offer. Consider returning to how you support a client's changes in Define Your Unique Value (p. 3).

Then, you might say, "Agile coach, focused on"

- Product-oriented teamwork
- More frequent releases that customers want
- Leadership teamwork

Even better, how can you explain what you do *without* using the term agile coach?

If you've started to write and speak, you can use: "Agile coach, blogging and speaking practical tips for" and then add the focus.

Make your headline inviting to your ideal clients, regardless of whether you're consulting yet. Here are three brief examples:

- Joe Jones, supporting teams' technical excellence. Joe clearly works at the team level.
- Felicity Fawn, expertise in creating both a humane culture and better business results.
- Joan Smith, building responsibility into product architecture.

Now write a brief bio.

4.2.2 *Write a Brief Bio to Attract Clients*

You will need a one-paragraph biography—bio—for your business. I use that same bio when I give talks, write articles, and on the About page on my site.

Because your bio connects the reader with the problems you solve, your bio starts building a relationship with your potential client. Help your client want you.

While resumes list each piece of your experience, a bio summarizes your expertise in a short form.

Here's my template for a one-paragraph bio:

- Line 1: Introduce you, as a consultant, to the reader. Use verbs. Allow that first sentence to invite your ideal client to read more or to have them choose not to work with you.
- Line 2: Summarize the changes you help your clients make.
- Line 3: Add some other form of expertise or credibility that helps the client see the benefits of working with you. This line might answer "why you" to a client.
- Line 4: If you have extensive experience, add this line as a "wow" factor.
- Line 5: At a minimum, direct people to your site.

Write a first draft of your bio. As you review it, check for jargon and remove that. Avoid passive voice, the "is" verbs. Always check your bio for readability so people can skim your bio.

Once you've consulted for a while, consider writing different bios for speaking, writing, and consulting. And if you choose to write books, create a longer bio that lists all the books.

You might discover, as I did, that LinkedIn substitutes for a resume. I no longer maintain a separate resume. Instead, I use LinkedIn for a much longer profile of my experience and skills.

While LinkedIn does substitute for a resume, always keep a copy of your online profiles. Keep your information even as sites change.

You might maintain a more extensive profile or resume with lists of skills or certifications. However, a bio is one paragraph of prose.

Here's my current bio:

- Line 1: Johanna Rothman, known as the "Pragmatic Manager," offers frank advice for your tough problems. (If they don't want frank advice, they don't want me.)
- Line 2: She helps leaders and teams learn to see simple and reasonable things that work. (A summary of how I work and who I work with.)
- Line 3: Equipped with that knowledge, they can decide how to adapt their product development. (My why and why they should work with me.)
- Line 4: Johanna is the author of eighteen books and hundreds of articles. (Not many people have written this much.)
- Line 5: Find the Pragmatic Manager, a monthly email newsletter, and her blogs at jrothman.com and createadaptablelife.com. (I want people to check my newsletter and read more.)

I use this initial paragraph for most of my bios. When I need a shorter bio, I keep Lines 1 and 5. Then, I decide what else to keep.

Don't let perfection get in the way of your progress. Expect to iterate on your bio for years. Write a good-enough bio that connects with your ideal clients.

4.2.3 *Use Your Bio to Connect*

Do you want to impress or connect with clients?

Several of my colleagues use their bios to impress their clients. I do include that Wow line in my bio. However, I have a guideline about what to put in my bio: Will this information connect with my ideal clients? If the information might push my ideal clients away, I don't include it.

If you work for a consulting firm—not as an independent consultant—you may need to add your degrees or certifications to your bio. I would call that a profile instead.

I don't list certifications because I no longer hold or believe in them. My content marketing proves my expertise, so my clients don't care.

I don't list degrees in *my* bio because that degree does not matter to any of my clients. However, your potential clients might need to know you have a degree. In that case, include the most relevant degree.

Avoid giving clients a reason to say "No" to you. One infamous client didn't read my bio but did review my degrees. He thought my Master's in Systems Engineering was about requirements.

After he finally contacted me, we laughed when I explained my degree was about how to engineer a product and its necessary social systems.

I've also worked with executives who didn't have degrees—and they were sensitive about that fact. Why would I push away an ideal client because I'm so impressed with myself?

Use your bio to connect with and attract clients, not push them away.

4.2.4 Draft Your First Bio

Try my one-paragraph bio template to write your bio. Open a new document of your choice, and write the template at the top.

Here's a way to practice:

- Part 1: Write your 5-line bio. Start with simple sentences—and as many sentences as you need for a line. Write down whatever you need to help connect with your potential clients.
- Part 2: Now, review the words you used. Do you have any "is" or "are" words? Change those to active verbs.
- Part 3: Review for "and" words. Split any sentence with an "and" into two sentences.
- Part 4: Run a grammar and spell checker. What's the reading ease and grade level? If your grade level is over grade 9, simplify the sentences. If the reading ease is under 60, consider simplifying the sentences.

Remember: it's a bio. It's not a resume with lists of skills. It's a 5-line prose introduction that helps your potential ideal client connect with you to build a relationship.

Iterate on your bio as much and as often as you like. Nobody knows or cares how much you need to iterate on your bio.

4.2.5 Describe What You Offer

Create a brief description of the benefits of working with you. Do not add your products and services. Limit this section to between 150-250 words.

Add links here to:

- Your website
- Your email newsletter
- Videos of you speaking
- Slide decks

Read what other consultants have here, and consider which consultants you want to copy. (Do not copy the text, but how they frame what they offer.) Iterate on that until you have the text good enough.

4.2.6 *Complete the Profile*

Since you did the work in Chapters 1 and 2, itemizing all the value you offer, you can add that information here, too.

Add all your work experiences.

How Many Years of Experience Should You List?

Ageism is alive and well when people look for employee roles. Too many hiring managers worry an "old" employee is too old.

However, you don't want to be an employee. You plan to work for yourself and use your experience to benefit your clients. In that case, your experience can serve you well.

That's why I recommend you include all your working years. If you have more than twenty years of experience, you might summarize the first ten or so years. In my profile, I use this sentence: "A variety of technical contributor roles in Engineering organizations."

Remember to add your publications, awards, and patents. It doesn't matter if those relate to your desired consulting role. Each of them contributes to how people see your professionalism.

4.3 Finish Preparation for Your Active Marketing Conversation

I also said you need these pieces in preparation for the conversation:

- A professional email address.
- A bio for talks you will propose. You can use the bio you drafted earlier in this chapter.

- A hi-res professional photo of you alone with a neutral background.
- A phone number you can use for your business calls.

With any luck, you already have these pieces in place. However, now is the time to verify you have what you need.

All this preparation leads us to the active marketing phone call.

4.4 Create Your Active Marketing Discussion Script

I create an active marketing "script." Even though I don't read from it, I write it down to know what I plan to say.

When I actively market, I have these objectives:

- Make sure you have five or ten minutes with this person.
- Briefly describe your business. You can use the brief description of your offer in Describe What You Offer (p. 61).
- Ask about what's happening with the other person. (This is a conversation.) As part of listening, offer value if you can.
- Ask for referrals, not work.
- Consider asking if they want to receive your email newsletter.
- Say thank you.

I offer this "script" to you as a starting point. Please put this in your own words.

1. Say hello and verify this is a good time to talk.
2. Explain you've started your consulting business (or you're changing your focus). You wanted to let this person know. *Briefly* explain the problems you solve.
3. Ask the other person, "How's your work going?" or "What's new with you?"
4. As you listen, take notes. You might have read something or know something that would benefit the other person. You can mention that here and say, "I'll email that to you, so you don't

have to write it down." Notice that you're offering value *before* you ask for anything.

5. Explain you'd love referrals for speaking opportunities and to other people who might benefit from your work. Then say, "If you know of anyone who could use me, please let me know. Thanks."

6. Explain that you write a newsletter. Ask if they would like to see an issue. Or ask if they would subscribe. (Never add anyone to your newsletter who does not explicitly request it.)

7. Say goodbye and thank them for their time.

Keep these calls to 10 minutes unless you're having a great conversation.

Follow up with a short email where you can send names of books or links to the reading you discussed in a follow-up email. Include a link to your email newsletter and ask them to subscribe.

4.5 Call—Not Email or Social Media

You might wonder why I recommend you call and not email.

A phone call encourages a short real-time conversation. You don't need to make an appointment, as you would for video, and you can keep the conversation to ten minutes or less.

And, if you're like me, you're less likely to contact someone you don't know. Stick with a phone call, and you'll likely spend the right amount of time.

I don't recommend you email people to make contact for these reasons:

- People quickly hit delete before reading what you wrote.
- You have to wait for them to respond. You don't have control over their actions—you only have control over your actions.
- When you speak with someone in real time, you reinforce the relationship you already have.

In addition, when you call, you can ask people to subscribe to your newsletter. Even though that's a small request, they might say no, and that's fine. You asked.

You might wonder if you can use social media, such as LinkedIn or Twitter, for your active marketing. You can write a post and publicize your new business on social media. However, since all social media decides who will see your posts, you can't know how many views that post will have. I do not recommend you use any form of social media to reinforce your existing relationship.

You can only start an effective business with other people's help and support. When you ask people for help, you tell them you have the emotional strength to realize that fact and that you're not afraid.

You might be surprised at how much people will help you.

Let's discuss how you might organize your active marketing actions for three months to find enough clients.

4.6 Call Everyone You Know

Who should you call? Everyone you know.

In the Introduction, I said that it took me three months to land my first engagement. I used a script similar to the one above and made a list of all the cards in my Rolodex. Yes, I am admitting my age.

Starting with the A last names, I called five people a day for three months. I even let my accountant, doctor, and dentist know I was now consulting. By the time I got to the L's, I had landed the first engagement. Then, my content marketing kicked in.

I suspected that some of the people in my Rolodex would say, "That's nice," and forget about me as soon as we stopped talking. However, one of them realized his loose connection was one of my potential clients. He made the call and referred me to my first client.

Keep an open mind about who you should call. Call everyone you know.

4.7 Plan for Three Months of Active Marketing

While this plan worked for me, this plan will not be perfect for you. However, there are principles that matter:

- In discussions, offer relevant and valuable content that relates to your unique expertise.
- Regularly add new people to your network.
- Write and speak wherever possible. People will more likely recognize you from your active marketing as you create your content marketing.
- Listen to the other person's reactions to your offerings as you use your active marketing script. If no one is excited about what you offer, that might be information you can use to hone the changes you want to help clients make.

Here's how you might organize your next three months. In addition, update the marketing plan you created in Create Your Marketing Plan (p. 44).

4.7.1 Month 1 Activities: Prepare for Success

You might want to separate these activities into "morning" and "afternoon." If you're like me, do the stuff you hate in the morning, and the work you enjoy in the afternoon.

Review all the activities in Chapters 1 and 2 of this book. Make sure you understand the value you offer to your ideal clients.

- Build your first draft online profile.
- Make sure you add connections and network with people.
- Attend meetups for two reasons aside from the content. Listen to how other consultants introduce themselves. And use those meetups to test your business. Say, "I'm considering consulting in this general area." Listen to any reactions.
- Generate titles and descriptions for at least two talks. Offer your talks to at least two meetups.

If you finish this before the month is over, start your active marketing conversations.

4.7.2 *Month 2 Activities: Network and Actively Market*

- Conduct at least five calls with connections each day. (Especially by Month 2, I hated calling, so I did that first.)
- As you listen to what people say on these calls, iterate on your products and services. Are you offering enough valuable benefits that ideal clients will buy something from you? I iterated on my products and services when I started my business.
- Offer to speak at professional groups.
- Write as often as you can to build your intellectual property.
- If you're like me, you'll iterate on your profile.

You might need these tips to make it easier for you to succeed:

- I made a list of the five people to call each day. I gathered their information and had it ready, along with my script.
- I made a list of groups I wanted to speak to and contacted one organizer a day.

Make the work easy so you can succeed at it.

4.7.3 *Month 3 Activities: Combine Active and Content Marketing*

Even if some clients have contacted you, continue these activities so you don't fall into the trap of just one client:

- Continue to call at least five people each day.
- Make your weekly content marketing more predictable: specific days or times. Readers will start to expect your content marketing.

Even with a free blog, ensure you have a sufficient web presence. See Define Your Web Presence and Email (p. 229).

If you still need to get consulting work, ask some recent connections about their challenges. Are you offering your services to people who can use them?

Even with content marketing, you might need to return to active marketing under these circumstances:

- When you *significantly* change what you offer. If your previous clients cannot use what you now offer, you might need both content and active marketing to attract your changed ideal clients.
- When the business world undergoes an unexpected contraction or recession.
- When your previous clients no longer need or want your services—and no one else does either.

As I said, I prefer content marketing over active marketing. However, if you need to find clients fast or the world changes, active marketing might be just what you need.

4.8 Active Marketing Until Clients Contact You

While I've offered guidelines for three months of active marketing, you might need more time until your content marketing helps clients contact you.

What if you obtain a large-enough client engagement in your first three months? Celebrate, deliver that engagement, and continue all your marketing. I recommend you move your focus to content marketing, while you continue to add people to your LinkedIn network.

Even if you can now focus on content marketing, remember to network and update your online presence. Beware the stop-start-stop problem of marketing. That's where you obtain a client engagement so you *stop* any marketing. Then you realize after that engagement you need to *start* marketing. Then you gain an engagement and *stop*.

Potential clients will forget you if you're not consistent.

4.9 Now Try This to Attract Clients with Active Marketing

I've suggested many activities throughout this chapter. Start here:

1. Start networking with people now. Remember to add people you met recently to your network.
2. Every time you go to a meetup, offer your LinkedIn profile and connect with others.
3. Write your bio. A first draft is fine, and continue to refine it to make it better.
4. Make sure your LinkedIn profile is complete.
5. Draft your active marketing script so you're comfortable talking to strangers or people you barely know. You could start with colleagues and ask them for help. Do they like what you say?
6. Start your content marketing even as you use active marketing. Even if you find a client, you still want that person to realize how valuable you are.

Consider that three-month active marketing plan.

Between your content marketing and active marketing, you have a client contact. Now, it's time to build the client relationship.

CHAPTER 5

Build the
Client Relationship

Content marketing initiates a relationship with potential clients because the content shows clients the changes they might expect. The more focused content you create, the more your content builds empathy and trust with these potential clients.

Once a potential client contacts you, you can reinforce that relationship.

While successful independent consultants will work with various people across an organization, only one type of buyer can fund a project. Learn to recognize which buyer type contacts you.

5.1 Recognize Your Buyer

In their classic book, *Strategic Selling: The Unique Sales System Proven Successful by America's Best Companies* MIH85, Miller and Heiman describe four kinds of buyers:

- Economic buyer: the person with the money to pay for the product or service.
- User buyer: The person who will use the product or service.
- Technical buyer: The person who judges the product's or service's value or worth.
- The buyer coach: the person who can help you meet the buyers in the organization.

The only person who can buy from you is the economic buyer.

Even if you aim your content marketing at the "right" people in the organization, those people are often busy. Instead, many successful consultants tend to interact with a technical or user buyer first. Here's an example from my business.

Abe, a project manager, or a senior technical person, realizes their projects aren't working the way he expects them to. Abe discovers me through my content marketing: an article, a blog post, or a talk. (I attract Abe with my expertise.)

Abe decides I might be someone worth knowing, so he reads more articles or blog posts. Abe suspects I can help with his problems. He subscribes to my newsletter. (I keep Abe with my drip content marketing.)

At some point, Abe reviews my website to see what I offer for his problems.

Abe decides he needs a custom workshop and wants me to develop and deliver that workshop. Since Abe plans to take that workshop, he contacts me. Now, Abe is both the user buyer and the technical buyer. However, Abe cannot spend any of the company's money. He's not the economic buyer.

Abe starts the process with an email to his director, Susan. He asks Susan to choose me to bring this workshop to the company. He sends several links to my blog, some articles, and a link to the workshop.

If Abe and I have already talked, he might also be the coach buyer to help Susan choose me.

Susan, the director, receives Abe's email. While Susan didn't know me before, she knows what she wants for project management training. Susan likes what she reads for content and the workshop. Based on my content, she thinks she wants me. However, Susan is not the economic buyer either. Mandy, the VP, is the only person who can buy. That makes Susan another technical buyer.

Susan can veto my work. She can't approve it—that's what makes her the technical buyer. Abe might still be a technical buyer, but that depends on what Mandy thinks of Abe.

Susan takes Abe's email, adds a few more links, and forwards that email to Mandy. Susan explains the outcomes she wants and says to Mandy, "We should ask her for a proposal."

Now, Mandy does some research, reading what Abe and Susan sent. My content marketing makes sense to her.

Notice that while Abe originally discovered me through content marketing, every successive person at the client browses more of my content. They decide I have enough expertise that they convince themselves I'm the right consultant for their organization.

Now, with any luck, Mandy and Susan discuss the outcomes they want. They want projects to finish faster and to rationalize the project portfolio. That's part of what I do, so their desired results match my skills. They might want more outcomes, but those are the two primary outcomes.

Mandy then asks Susan to set up a meeting with me and request a proposal.

In my discovery call, I realize Susan is not the economic buyer. I ask her for a discovery call with Mandy. I use phrases such as "clarify the outcomes you want" and "determine any upper bounds for the work, so I don't offer something that's not right."

Because I ask Susan to organize the call, Susan becomes my coach buyer in addition to her role as the technical buyer. Abe might still be a coach buyer, but because Susan has more hierarchical clout, she's the primary coach and technical buyer.

However, only Mandy is the economic buyer.

Too often, consultants receive calls from fake economic buyers. These people mean well and want to do a great job, but they can't buy from you (or sign a purchase order).

5.2 Beware of Fake Economic Buyers

Many of my clients find me the way Abe found me. However, not all conversations work through the various technical or user buyers to the economic buyer. Many of my clients insert a fake economic buyer in the middle of the discussions.

Those clients have policies that drive their procurement. A specific functional group, such as HR (Human Resources) or Corporate

Learning, is supposed to source and verify a consultant's ability to do the job.

The HR or Learning department people have terrific intentions. However, they do *not* own the outcomes that the economic buyer wants. Nor do they understand the technical buyers' needs. That's because they don't understand the underlying issues that prevent the economic buyer from achieving those desired outcomes.

HR or the Learning departments only know how to evaluate you in only one dimension—your fee.

Treat these people with respect. And say something like this: "I would do you a disservice if I didn't speak to the person who needs the outcomes. Otherwise, we're playing 'telephone,' and I might misunderstand what you want. I'm happy to book an hour any time to speak with the person with the real needs."

All fake economic buyers can do is say No to your work. Their Yes only means they don't find you offensive. Their No removes you from consideration. They are fake economic buyers—even if the corporate money flows through them. That's because *they* don't have the problems you can solve.

I Learned the Hard Way Who the Buyer Really Was

After a conference talk, I met Jim, whose card said, "Director." We spoke several times during the conference, and he decided he wanted to discuss a workshop for his team.

When I returned home, I sent Jim a syllabus, and he loved it. We iterated on it, and I asked, "So, how about a purchase order?"

He said, "I don't have signature authority over $3500. You need to talk to my boss."

Oh. I spent all that time with a person who was both the technical and user buyer. I still needed to speak to the economic buyer. I said, "Okay, I'd like your assistance connecting with your boss."

He said, "I can't do that. She's a very busy person."

Uh oh. Jim wasn't going to be my coach buyer either. I asked, "How about you try, anyway?"

He did make the introductions. I thanked him. I sent Jim's boss a private email and said, "I hear you might have these problems. If you do, I can help."

She said, "Thanks and no thanks."

I didn't realize then, but she added herself to my email newsletter. Four years later, at a different company, she called me and said, "Let's talk."

I wasted too much time with Jim because I didn't ask enough questions. However, I did get the referral to the economic buyer and got lucky later.

—An experienced consultant

While your coach or technical buyer sees problems, they can't pay for your services. And until the economic buyer feels those problems, they won't buy from you.

That's when it's worth asking if the coach or technical buyer can be an economic buyer for a much smaller engagement. You can help them explain why they need a more extensive engagement in the future.

But HR and Learning (or other workgroups) aren't the only fake economic buyers. Sometimes, Purchasing, Procurement, or Contracting are also fake economic buyers. These people often have some link to money or contracts in their name.

I learned this—again—the hard way. I had negotiated both a fee and payment terms with a large company. However, the economic buyer only agreed to the fee. The contracting person had to agree to the negotiated payment terms instead of his. And his terms were nothing I had negotiated.

We took a month to agree on both the fee and the terms. And at one point, I offered to walk away from the engagement. (In the end, I got the terms I had negotiated, but it took a month. I increased my fee for the next engagement.)

Fake economic buyers exist everywhere. Here's the one question you can ask to see if you're dealing with a fake economic buyer:

Can this person say yes to an engagement?

If this person can only say no, that person is a fake economic buyer.

These fake economic buyers are not bad people because they want to save the company money. However, the fake economic buyers only see the *costs* of working with you. In contrast, the economic buyer sees the *value* of working with you.

Sometimes, your content marketing reaches the economic buyer first. But, since you can't depend on that, learn to recognize the economic buyer for this opportunity. A real-time conversation, in the form of a discovery call, will help you understand who is who.

But what if you're asked to respond to an RFP instead of a conversation? You get to decide.

5.3 Decide How You Will Respond to RFPs

An RFP is a "Request for Proposal." I've seen companies use RFPs badly in at least these ways: to "objectively" evaluate several consultants, to find a consultant's "best" fee, or to eliminate the need for a discovery call.

First is the evaluation problem. That's where the leaders who have this problem think they can reduce a trust-based relationship to totally quantifiable questions.

Worse, the RFP confuses the economic and technical buyer positions. The person who calls you *should* be the economic buyer. In reality, this person is the technical buyer. They relinquished their power to the person who manages the RFP.

In this case, you meet a potential client, Tom. Tom says he loves your work and wants to hire you. However, Tom's company feels they must evaluate several consultants, and they want you to respond to an RFP. You hit it off with Tom, so you start to fill out the RFP. That's when you realize you need more information. Based on your conversations with Tom, the RFP description is insufficient to help Tom and his department change.

Do you ask the potential client to change the RFP? Do you offer something less than what the client needs? Do you decide to ask for changes later?

The leaders don't want you to ask those questions—that's why they created the RFP.

It could be another, sometimes, related problem. The leaders want to spend less money solving this problem. So they ask for sealed bids (you're not supposed to know who your competition is or what they propose). You offer your best fee. When they awarded the contract, they chose the lowest bid, not the fairest fee—even if it was just a few thousand dollars below your fee.

I've also seen companies use RFPs to eliminate the need for a discovery call. The client does want you. But they think a discovery call is a "waste of time." These organizations believe they are saving time by reducing the relationship-building time you need with your client.

In each case, the client company shortcuts the necessary trust-building consultants need to help the client change.

That's why I never respond to RFPs. Not even when the client says, "I already decided on you." Sometimes, I ask, "Is there anyone who can veto your decision?" I might respond if the answer is no, and I want to work with this client. However, I include an additional paperwork fee for the aggravation of typing all my proposal information into their format.

But, I often discover that, yes, there is someone who can veto the client's decision.

Only you can decide whether responding to an RFP is worth your time. But even if you choose to respond to an RFP, you'll still need to build a trusting, empathetic relationship with your client.

I strongly recommend you use a discovery call to build trust.

5.4 Set the Context for Trust with a Discovery Call

As you speak with the economic buyer, you build trust with that person. The discovery call uses a three-part approach to create trust as the basis for a successful engagement:

- As you learn the signals the client sees, clarify the context, so the two of you can explore the reasons for those signals.
- Based on that context, discuss the boundaries of the problems they want you to solve—and whether you want to accept those boundaries.
- Discuss possible outcomes and engagement alternatives so you can both succeed.

As you use active listening skills, you and the client learn to trust each other. And you can verify that, yes, you are speaking with the economic buyer.

The discovery call will help you learn about the person, their challenges, and the outcomes they want to achieve. In addition, you'll determine if you want to work with this potential client.

5.5 Learn with a Discovery Call

I'm calling this interaction a "call," but you can use any mode you like—as long as you use real-time communication. I'm more likely to use video instead of a phone because I can build empathy and rapport faster with video.

Email is the Wrong Tool for Discovery

I receive too many emails, starting with, "We have these problems. We want to hire you. How much will it be?"

My ego loves those emails. My business mind says, "Uh oh." Often, the sender does describe problems where I can help. And I'm worried about moving to an answer about the client's needs without a discovery call.

Discovery calls help me build rapport. In addition, I learn the boundaries of the problems and what the client perceives as constraints. Because I show my expertise, I rarely look like a commodity to my clients. Discovery calls help me differentiate my unique expertise. And because I'm showcasing my expertise, no one questions my fees.

I use the discovery call to see if I can or want to work with this client—or if I want to refer this work to someone else.

Discovery calls help me envision the client's environment and offer me early warning signs:

- Clients who worry about fees might want you to offer them a rough, ballpark estimate for this work in the call. However, too often, those clients want to pay by the hour. Paying for expertise by the hour creates an untrusting dynamic because the client wants as little time as possible, while the consultant wants as much time as possible.
- When potential clients say they feel so much pressure that they don't want to take the time to discuss the issues, I offer a trusted advisor engagement. Often, that's the support they need to move away from all their pressure. However, I'm reluctant to offer any other alternative because I need to determine what the client wants or needs.

The discovery call fulfills two essential functions:

1. Learn about the client's unique context, and
2. Continue to help the client understand why I am the right consultant for their challenges.

The more I learn about the client's context, the easier it is to generate options for possible solutions.

And when I use active listening to learn and build respect, the more likely the client wants to work with me. The client and I build rapport and trust.

Once I understand their context, I can decide if I'm the right consultant for their needs.

5.5.1 *Clarify the Client's Context*

When a client calls, I start with their context. I have these goals for the discovery call:

- Learn about the client's organizations and honor the client's observations and experience.
- Expose their boundaries and constraints.
- Explore possibilities for collaboration with options.

I generally plan on about 20 minutes for each of these goals. If we use all our time on the first two of these, I offer collaboration possibilities via email and have another meeting.

I take notes to clarify the context and use active listening techniques.

When I use video for a discovery call, I explain I'm taking notes electronically. I say, "You might hear me typing, and I might look as if I'm looking off to the side because I'm taking notes."

I take notes to gather all the details, large and small, as the client explains what they see and hear. Many times, the client has already decided what the problem is. That's because the client sees the pain or symptoms of the problem, not the root causes. Sometimes, the client has already decided what the solution needs to be.

That's when I say, "Good. Let me understand more of the boundaries, constraints, and causes of those problems before we go for a solution."

That's when I ask questions about various circumstances where they see this problem. I use several listening and questioning techniques to elicit these answers:

- What do you *see* when this problem occurs?
- What do you *hear* when this problem occurs?
- What outcomes do you want?

I use these interviewing techniques to understand all the possible symptoms and causes. This call helps me see the extent of their problems.

I aim to create the outcomes with the client, especially to define the value they want from this project. At the end of the context section of the discovery call, I know this data: a ballpark of how much it costs them to work their current way and the outcomes they want. This data answers the first two items in Start with This Proposal Template (p. 89).

Now, it's time to see the boundaries and constraints, especially for time and money.

5.5.2 *Expose the Boundaries and Constraints*

I prefer to start this part of the call by discussing the organizational realities. However, sometimes, the client approaches me with a particular solution in mind. They might worry about my availability or the cost of the project. That's when I ask,

- Do you have a monetary upper bound for this project?
- Do you have a timeframe in mind?

If they have boundaries and I know I'm not interested in working within those bounds, I Decline the Work (p. 85).

If the client says they don't know about any monetary upper bound, I ask if they can make the buying decision. If not, this person might be a coach or technical buyer.

Avoid spending time with people who aren't the economic buyer. Only the economic buyer knows their desired outcomes and their perceived value for those outcomes.

However, the coach or technical buyer might help me generate options I can use later.

Let's assume I am speaking with the economic buyer. In that case, with an upper monetary bound, I might offer proposal stages. For example, one client, Sam, wanted an assessment, a custom workshop based on the assessment findings, and ongoing coaching. However, when we discussed my fee, Sam said he couldn't get that much money *now*.

Instead, I wrote a proposal for each item separately. Sam could say, "This is enough for now," and we could proceed.

If a client has a time constraint, such as needing to spend money before the end of the year, we negotiate what I can deliver and when.

Money and time are just two organizational boundaries and constraints. You might also discover there are people you must avoid. As you learn about the boundaries and constraints, decide if you want to adjust the outcomes for this engagement.

Some clients want to create insular engagements, eliminating the people we need for the desired outcomes. For example, some clients tell me my proposal can't involve finance, HR, product people, or anyone else who would be integral to the project's success.

In that case, I explain the outcomes we can achieve and those in doubt.

As you explore these various boundaries and constraints, you can create possible options, managing risk from this first call. Successful independent consultants share the risks and the rewards, collaborating to achieve success.

Now, it's time to explore the various possibilities.

5.5.3 *Explore Possible Options*

The last piece of the discovery call is when we explore options. The client probably had a specific option in mind, such as a workshop.

Given the client's context, boundaries and constraints, and desired outcomes, I might want to suggest alternatives.

Let the outcomes drive your option exploration. Remember to write the options down as you proceed. I often say, "I want to make sure I write this down so I don't forget something important."

Then, I generate three options to test what the client wants and does not want. As I offer options, I explain the outcomes I suspect the client will get from each option.

I then offer three options on the call. As I offer the options, I explain which outcomes the client can obtain from each possibility. Once we agree on the options, I say, "I'll write a proposal. If you realize you want something different, we can iterate. That's why I write proposals—so we can iterate on the proposal."

Do not discuss fees as you generate options. As you examine the options, the outcomes might change, which means the fees will change. For example, "This alternative might solve outcomes one and two, but not outcome three."

When the client pushes me to a ballpark estimate, I say, "I haven't thought these options through yet, so I can't offer you a fair fee." Then I clarify their monetary bounds again to make sure we both understand.

Why Offer Three Alternatives?

I use Weinberg's Rule of Three to help my clients. One solution is a trap. Two alternatives create a dilemma—which option could you choose? Three options help the client—and me—create even better alternatives. I use the Rule of Three in many aspects of my business.

Even better, clients need to see the three alternatives so they anchor themselves. When I offer three options, each with its fee, the client often selects the middle option.

If the client isn't sure, even at the end of this call, you have alternatives:

- Email the client over three or four days. Then, write a proposal.
- Set a time and date *this week* for another call. Remind the client that the only agenda item is to generate options.
- Offer to perform a short paid assessment so that you can guide the client's thinking.

Consider creating project-based fees for services such as workshops. That will allow you to say, "In general, workshops for twelve people range from x to y." Make sure the x, the lowest amount, is your regular workshop fee.

Now it's time to agree on the next steps.

5.5.4 *Wrap the Call with an Agreement*

Finish the call with as much agreement as possible. Here are things the client and the consultant can agree on:

- The options the consultant will explain in the proposal, including the client and consultant's responsibilities.
- The date the consultant will send the proposal.
- When the client will respond to the proposal.

That agreement helps you write the proposal.

You've now gained agreement—in principle—for everything in the proposal.

5.6 Gain Agreement Before You Write a Proposal

Successful consultants keep this goal in mind for a discovery call: keep the client saying yes.

- Start that agreement with the signals and problems, and continue with the causes.
- Then, gain agreement on what it costs the client to continue to work this way and the value of the benefits.
- Finally, explore possibilities.

Use the discovery call to be most effective in a reasonable amount of time.

Keep these two ideas in mind in the context of a discovery call, so you don't blame the client for their current situation:

Batalden's quote: "*Every system is perfectly designed to get the results it gets.*"

Weinberg's quote: "*No matter what it looks at first, it's always a people problem.*"

These quotes can put you in a frame of mind that might help you create options in a proposal that allows the client to see and change their system.

I sometimes test alternatives with the client. I might ask this question, "So, maybe a mini-assessment which will inform a custom workshop?"

5.7 Decline the Work

You don't have to do all the work you *can*, especially if the client creates constraints or you realize you no longer want to do that work.

For example, one client wanted me to "train" 50 people by phone for an hour. But the outcomes they wanted only matched an on-site several-day workshop. Their self-imposed constraints prevented any possible success. You can say, "I excel at the outcomes you want. However, I don't know how to deliver the outcomes you want with these constraints. My best wishes to you." I mean the part about best wishes.

And sometimes, as you work through the discovery call, you realize you don't look forward to this work. That's a sign that you can drop that work and refer other consultants to the client. I say, "I no longer do that work. Here are three other consultants you should know about."

What if you worry you don't have the expertise for *this* engagement? Always tell the truth. If you want to *gain* this expertise, explain that you and the client will learn together. Or, you might refer the client to someone else.

However, if your expertise does not match the client's current needs, explain you are not the right consultant for them.

I always ask the client to stay in touch and sign up for my email newsletter. I don't burn bridges.

5.8 Respect the Client

In this chapter, I've suggested ways you might put your respect for the client into practice. I've recommended the following:

- Using empathy to see the client's concerns.
- Keep an open mind during the discovery call.
- Learn about the client's context, boundaries, and constraints with a discovery call.
- Explore alternatives with the client.
- Understand when you are not suitable for this client.

If you do this, you and the client will build mutual respect. You can suggest several alternatives, and the client will be happy to discuss them with you. And, the more the client respects you, the more value you can offer. With more respect, you can create a fee structure the client will appreciate.

Sometimes, consultants ask me what to do if they *know* the solution on the discovery call. And it's a small thing, but something the client can use to start a successful change. What should they do? One of these consultants said, "It's like seeing a car with a flat tire. You can't *not* tell the client, can you?"

Of course not. Respectfully tell the client: "Looks to me as if you have a flat tire on the back passenger side of the car. Did you check that tire?"

If the client says, "Oh, thank you!" you might be done with *this* problem. Consider explaining the value of your observation. For example, you might say, "I suspect that flat tire is costing you about a person-week a month. Please do fix that flat. I'll check back with you in a month and see if the flat tire was your only problem."

As Weinberg said in *Secrets of Consulting* WCO14:

"Once you eliminate your number one problem, number two gets a promotion."

Ask the person if you can add them to your newsletter, and check back in a month.

Because you treated them respectfully and called back later, they will want to engage you to solve their *next* problem. Every time I did this, the next problem was much more complex and something I wanted to work on with the client.

5.9 Now Do This to Build Your Client Relationships

In your consulting notebook, write down these questions and your answers.

If you are a consultant, consider your most recent three clients and answer these questions. If you're still an employee, answer these questions thinking about a more senior person in your organization.

1. How many ways do you currently recognize the economic buyer, the person who can say yes to spending time or money to solve a problem?
2. Which active listening and interviewing skills have you practiced in the last month? What have you learned from recent conversations that appeared to go astray where you did not influence the outcome?

3. Think of three successful conversations where you discussed options and agreed with a manager more senior to you.
4. When have you been pleasantly surprised when you considered new options? When have you been unpleasantly surprised?

Now that you've started building that client relationship, you can create a proposal.

CHAPTER 6

Create Successful Proposals

You've completed the discovery call and discussed three options the client likes. Now it's time to write a proposal.

The proposal organizes and clarifies the details of the discovery call. The details include your reflections on the current client state, the value of each alternative, and your fee.

Consider this proposal template to organize these details.

6.1 Start with This Proposal Template

In the discovery call, you focused on helping the client say "yes" to the situation and possible alternatives. That includes the client's current state, the client's desired outcomes, and your three alternatives to achieve those outcomes.

Proposals are a solidification of the conversations, not marketing. (See Alan Weiss' *Million Dollar Consulting: The Professional's Guide to Growing a Practice* WEI16 for that gem as well as many others.)

I modified Weiss's template for my consulting practice. Here's my proposal template with explanations:

1. Summary of the current situation. In one or two paragraphs, explain the client's current state. Include the costs of how the client works now. Those costs are tangible and support your fees.

2. The outcomes—the changes or explanations—the client wants. Change-based outcomes, such as workshops or coaching, affect a client's revenue or costs. Explanation-

based outcomes, such as from an assessment, support the client's next steps.

3. Measures to show progress or completion. As a guideline, only use progress measures if this work is at least a month in duration. Do not use this for Trusted Advisor work, because that's access to you, not outcome-based.

4. Value the client can expect. As a guideline, consider generating at least three tangible and intangible values for each outcome.

5. Three alternative options for the work. Organize each option in increasing cost and value. Also, explain the duration of each option.

6. The consultant's responsibilities. List your actions and expected outcomes.

7. The client's responsibilities. Consider a private workshop as an example. Who will invite the people and provide the space (virtual or face-to-face) for the work? List specific people or the responsibilities of people involved.

8. Terms and conditions: Specify a fee with terms for each option. For example, ask for a 50% deposit to hold the date for a workshop. You might choose to offer a five or ten percent discount for payment in full ten days before your work starts. Always clarify your fee with specific terms.

9. Explain how long this proposal is valid. Do you want a client to return to you in a year and ask you to honor a year-ago proposal? I use this line: "This proposal is valid for sixty days."

10. Add a signature line for the client to sign immediately. Very few of my clients are able to sign immediately, but maybe yours can.

11. Add a copyright line that has the phrase, "for internal name-of-the-client use only." You spent this time and energy customizing your proposal. You can't prevent a client from sharing your proposal with others, but you might help them reconsider. Some clients see more value in the proposal when they see your copyright statement.

Email the proposal as a pdf. If you are open to iterating the proposal, say that in your email.

That's the entire template. Now, let's start with the situation.

6.2 Summarize the Client's Situation and Outcomes

The first part of the discovery call clarified the client's context. Now, summarize that context. Include the signals the client sees.

The second part of the discovery call discussed the various boundaries of the work. Clarify those boundaries here. I rarely include any monetary boundaries, but I do include the scope of the work. Explain who you plan to work with and at what level.

Keep the situation to about two paragraphs. The client wants to see your options and fees, so clarify, but don't specify all the root causes.

Add one more paragraph about the outcomes the client desires. The desired outcomes drive your descriptions of the value.

6.3 Clarify the Value in the Proposal

While clients see signals, they might not see the tangible and intangible benefits for their desired outcomes.

The tangible benefits have two parts: the current waste that the client has now, and the future benefits the client can realize. For example, consultants can discuss these costs to create tangible benefits:

- Time-based delays: What kinds of delays does the client experience now? Describe the delays and the impact those delays have on which people and departments. Sometimes, the client does not realize delays cause people to leave the organization.
- Waste: What kinds of waste does the client experience? Waste often has impact around the signals the client sees. Given your current knowledge, estimate the kinds of waste you expect the client has.

- Friction: Waste often leads to friction within the organization. However, you might probe a little on customer friction. Start with tangible benefits when you assess friction. However, add in the intangible benefits, especially for customer-based friction.

The intangible benefits are how people will *feel* after you complete your work. And if you don't articulate the value *you* bring, the client might not realize the best possible outcomes. Ask the client how they expect people to *feel* after you deliver their desired outcomes. Those people might include the client's managers, staff, customers, and anyone else you will encounter during this work.

Use both the tangible and intangible benefits to create a reasonable project or value-based fee for this engagement.

I iterate over my proposals, clarifying the tangible and intangible benefits. That helps me clarify the options and the fees I associate with each option. You might choose to iterate, also.

6.4 Clarify the Client's Options

During the discovery call, you and the client explored possible options. Now, it's time to write down those options.

Offer the client three options. Why three? Because the first one creates an anchoring effect. Daniel Kahneman, the behavioral economist, has written about anchoring bias in *Thinking Fast and Slow* KAH11.

The first number or the first option a person sees anchors them to the following options. That's why it helps you and your client to organize the options from least value and cost to greatest value and cost.

Write down the options first from least to greatest value.

Now that you see how the proposal fits together, send the proposal to the client quickly.

6.5 Use Time as Your Advantage

The longer it takes a potential client to see your proposal, the longer that client can talk him or herself out of the need for *you* to do the work.

Don't allow your clients to second-guess themselves.

Write the proposal as soon as you end the discovery call and explain when the client can expect to receive your proposal. I recommend you aim for not more than two days between the end of the discovery call and when you send the proposal. That allows you to use time as an advantage with this client.

What if you're quite busy? Explain your time constraints and when you will start writing. With this template and a good discovery call, you can write a proposal within a few hours.

Sometimes, as I work through the alternatives and the fees, I realize the work is more extensive than either of us expected. In that case, I might ask the client for another call. I walk the client through my thinking and make sure the client doesn't have any objections. Are there organizational bounds I cannot cross?

Sometimes, I misunderstood the client's objectives. In that case, maybe the work is smaller than I thought. I often discover the client feels the work should take less time than I think it does. I use this second call to help the client see my concerns.

Even with this approach, I've seen proposal problems.

6.6 Fix Common Proposal Problems

I've outlined the way I create proposals:

1. Conduct a discovery call. Gain agreement on challenges, outcomes, and possible alternatives.
2. Create the proposal and send it within 48 hours or as early as possible, given my other work.
3. If the client realizes we missed challenges in the situation or outcomes, discuss them and update the proposal.

In the best possible world, we agree to the proposal. Or, I decline the work.

What if the client wants you to change something about the proposal?

And I remember what Gerald M. Weinberg, famous writer and consultant, said to me years ago:

"As the contracting goes—so goes the contract."

If you have trouble in the discovery call or proposal stage, you can expect similar problems in the actual work.

I've seen these proposal problems:

- The client wants you to change your fees because they "can't afford" your fees.
- The client has "standard terms" that might cause you to lose sleep over your cash flow.
- As I review my notes, I realize the client and I disagree on the outcomes, risks, or the work I think the client needs.
- Late-responding clients.

Let's start with the discovery call problem.

6.6.1 *Trap: No Time for a Discovery Call*

You receive a call from a potential client. They have five minutes to speak with you *right now*. Luckily, you have five minutes *right now*.

You spend those five minutes. You don't have enough information. The client then wants a ballpark estimate of the time and cost for what they think you can do to solve their problem. The client might even say, "I really need *you* to solve this problem."

Doesn't that sound wonderful? The client wants *you*. Don't be fooled—the client doesn't know the outcomes they need. You can't succeed.

I often choose one of these three responses in this situation:

- "I don't yet understand your outcomes. Since I need to understand them, and you're in a rush, can you deputize someone to speak with me? Or can you invest some time with me during the next couple of days? Or, I can create a retainer agreement if you know you want me and don't yet know the outcomes."

- "I can give you a ballpark. It's almost certain I will offer you the wrong solution for your problem. And, I will need to create a ballpark figure that's much more expensive than you probably expect. That's because I'm assuming all the risks for the outcomes you want." I often offer a ballpark that starts at twice my regular fee for what I think the work is. "If you can spend a total of an hour with me, I can offer you at least three alternatives that will work better."

- If I tried the other two responses, I then say, "I'm glad you called me. And, I don't work with clients who can't take the time to talk with me upfront about the benefits and outcomes they want. I wish you the best."

I can always offer three reasonable alternatives in a proposal *after* I speak with the client for an hour. I might not need an entire hour, but I always need at least 20 minutes.

If you let a client rush you to their preferred solution, neither you nor the client will benefit from the engagement.

What happens when I double the ballpark figure for a specific product or service, and the client pays it? I make enough money off this one engagement that I can learn from the client's real issues. I profit in terms of my learning and money. The client gets what the client asked for, even if it's not what the client needs.

I can be sure I won't receive a testimonial or a referral from that client—so I better make enough money this one time. I'll discuss this more in how you set fees, but I use the principle of "I want to be happy if I do or don't get the business."

Your client might be willing to discuss their issues with you. However, they think your fee is too high.

6.6.2 Trap: "You're Too Expensive"

Several clients have told me my proposal was "too expensive." Even after I determined these people were the genuine economic buyers. They had several reasons for that:

- They had no experience with consultants. They only understood hourly contractor rates.
- I hadn't shown my value in ways they could understand. Every time, I missed the intangible benefits.
- A couple of times, I hadn't understood the outcomes the client wanted.

When I had the consultant vs. contractor discussion with a potential client, they said, "We never pay that much to anyone who isn't a senior manager."

I explained I was the equivalent of a senior manager. I had the experience. Based on that experience, I could help them achieve their desired results faster than a less expensive consultant could.

This client didn't like my fee. First, they took the number of contact hours they thought I would use. Then, they divided my fee by the contact hours and calculated my "hourly" price.

That hourly fee was "too high."

I suggested the first alternative, which was a lower fee for less client value. That's when one of the people on the call said, "That's an even higher hourly rate."

I explained I don't charge by the hour. I only charge by the project. We continued to go back and forth. I finally realized that the client could only see the calculated hourly fee. That's not how I work. I use value to price my work.

I said, "While I can help you realize the outcomes you want, I am not a contractor, trading time for money. That's not in our best interests. So, calculating my hourly rate doesn't make sense. Therefore, I am not the consultant for you." (Yes, I recommend you say something like this.)

I wished them well.

When another client said, "You're too expensive," I asked, "Compared to what or whom? Compared to what you're losing every week with all your delays?"

Now, we could have a conversation about the value of the work.

Sometimes, even with a discovery call, I don't understand the outcomes the client wants. Often, that occurs when the person doesn't understand all the forces keeping the problems in place. Usually, that lack of understanding is because the person on the phone is not the economic buyer—even though the person had a senior-sounding title.

6.6.3 *Trap: Payment Terms Mismatch*

More and more of my clients have standard terms that pay invoices 60 or 90 days from the date of the invoice. I no longer take those payment terms. You don't have to take those terms, either.

It seems that the larger, well-known, and well-capitalized the company, the more oppressive their standard terms. If the client wants to know my fee when we discuss alternatives, I explain that my fees always include specific payment terms.

Sometimes, the buyer ignores the terms I included in the proposal. We don't see the mismatch until the Purchasing Department creates a Purchase Order. While the Purchasing department might ask for those terms—or even tell you that those are the standard terms, you have at least these choices:

- Ask the economic buyer to negotiate those terms.
- Explain to the economic buyer that you need to revisit the proposed fee because their terms are not what you expected.
- Decline the engagement.

You always get to decide if you want to take your client's terms. If you do take those terms, the client manages your cash flow. See Don't Let Your Clients Manage Your Money (p. 183) for more information.

Include your payment terms as part of your negotiation process for the options in your proposal.

I now ask clients what their standard terms are in the discovery call, so I understand what they expect for payment. If I don't like their standard terms, I can increase my fee.

Other consultants add a "Standard Paperwork Fee" to their proposals. Instead, consider offering a higher fee to offset the payment terms problems and to offer one or two possible discounts for earlier payment.

6.6.4 *Trap: We Differ on the Outcomes*

Sometimes, as I review my notes, I realize the client and I don't agree on the outcomes, risks, or the work the client needs. That's when I send an email to check with the client. In that email, I might offer to take another half-hour to walk through my concerns.

Not all clients want that extra time. That's when I tend to avoid working with this client.

As a successful consultant, I choose to work with clients who value my advice, starting with the proposal.

6.6.5 *Trap: Clients Respond Later Than You Expect*

You sent the proposal and said you'd check back with the client on a specific day. When I send a proposal, I often include a sentence such as this: "I'll check back with you on such-and-such a day if I don't hear from you before."

Some clients don't respond then—and worse, some of them never respond at all.

If a client doesn't respond, I often check in with them one more time, to make sure my email went through. But if they still don't respond, I assume they are not going to do so.

Then there are the clients who wait for six months and want to start an engagement next week. I explain that the proposal was good for two months and I ask to verify that the situation remains the same. Sometimes, it does. But these clients tend to be a challenge to work with. "As the contracting goes, so does the contract."

You don't have to take this client after they wait for six months to respond to you.

6.7 Decline the Work When It Doesn't Fit

Sometimes, even if you create a proposal you think is a good deal for both you and the client, you then realize it's not a good deal for either of you.

Several years ago, I served an ongoing client that liked many of my workshops. Unfortunately, they had a senior management change, and the new IT Vice President decided he would standardize on a particular framework.

He asked me for a proposal to "move" (his word) the entire 100+ person department to this framework in under six weeks. He also wanted me to coach the managers.

When I returned the proposal to him and asked for his feedback, he sounded offended. "You really think you can charge us this much money?"

I thought I'd stepped into the "too expensive" argument. I said, "Well, you want these outcomes, right?"

"No," he said, "I know you can do all this work within two hours a day, a couple of days a week."

I said, "I don't know how to help you achieve the outcomes you say you want in that amount of time. I can offer you this," and then gave him a different alternative.

"You're just rude!" he said and hung up on me. I'm happy I didn't say yes to that engagement. I never returned to that client, which I find disappointing. But, I don't have the aggravation of working in a no-win situation.

He wanted me to work for his benefit, not for our mutual benefit.

6.8 Check That the Proposal Offers Benefits to Both Parties

Before you send a proposal, check that the outcomes offer enough benefits to both you and the client. If the outcomes are too small, or the fee you can charge is too low, chances are good that the proposal doesn't offer enough value for both you and the client.

For example, some potential clients want a "one-hour speech" or "one hour of coaching." The client thinks these requests are small.

However, I have yet to do a "one-hour" anything that does not require preparation. The client might not *see* my preparation, but I do spend the time.

Think of all work this way: how much preparation work do you need to do to deliver the work? Is there any post-delivery work? Then, include all that time in your proposal and fee.

I use these guidelines for my proposals:

- Is it worth my time to write the proposal? If the work is not worth the time, I might work with the client to increase the value. However, I won't write a proposal for low fee work.
- Will both the client and I gain value from the proposed work?

I don't propose work that will cost me more to deliver than the value I gain in return.

Sometimes, the client doesn't have specific outcomes, but knows they want you. That's when you can create a retainer agreement. My retainer agreements are a little different from my proposals.

6.9 Create a Trusted Advisor Retainer Agreement

When I write outcome-based proposals, the client and I can agree on the outcomes, and any measures to assess the progress toward those outcomes.

However, not all clients know what they want. They know they want access to me. They are sure they need me, but not how much.

That's when I create a trusted advisor agreement based on a retainer. Trusted advisor agreements do not specify outcomes. They specify access to the consultant. However, you can't be totally available to the client any time of the day or night. That's why trusted advisor agreements need boundaries.

Here are some possible boundaries:

- Who can contact you? Just the client? A client's team? Someone who is a peer of the client?
- When can the client contact you? Are there times inside and outside of your regular business hours?
- How quickly will you respond? Do you need to respond within an hour, a day, a week? What if you are on vacation or traveling internationally?
- Will you have a set time each week to check in with the client? Some trusted advisor agreements look more like coaching, where the consultant periodically checks in with the client.
- How long does the agreement last? Decide how long the initial agreement will last. Clarify boundaries around renewals of this agreement and the fee for a renewal.
- How much time will you spend with the client weekly? Are there signals that mean the client needs something different from me?

Consider a retainer agreement with a minimum duration of one quarter and a maximum of one year, renewable for the same time at the same rate.

A retainer agreement is different from a coaching agreement, where the client might use all their sessions. As a trusted advisor with a retainer agreement, the consultant's time does not roll over from week to week, month to month, or quarter to quarter.

The client pays—in advance—for access to you. If the client does not use you in the time bounds for this retainer agreement, they lose that access. Consider if you want to check in with your client from time to time. But do not take care of your client. Trusted advisor work is about access to you.

Once you've sent the proposal, make sure the proposal does not go into the great bitbucket in the sky.

6.10 Track the Proposal

When you send a proposal, explain when you will check in with the client to see what they think.

I recommend checking in with the client in seven days—a week—to see what they think. Do not allow the client to take more time than that. If they can't respond in a week, discover if something happened. The client might want to iterate on the proposal with you. Your discussion of tangible and intangible benefits, along with your options, might trigger the client to consider even more work for you. That's terrific.

However, I often learn that the client has organizational changes that make it difficult for them to say yes to my proposal.

Here are problem I've seen when the proposal appears to go off to the bitbucket in the sky:

- The organization is going through change.
- The buyer's role changes.
- The client wants you to start and not wait for a PO.

Let's start with the client's organizational changes.

6.10.1 Learn about Organizational Changes

The client contacted you because the client saw problems. Sometimes, the organization creates changes that means your proposal no longer fits their context.

Some changes I've seen:

- Reorganization, where my client is no longer responsible for what we discussed. That person is no longer the economic buyer.

- Economic authority change, where the economic buyer has much less funding authority.
- Title-based authority change: A new senior manager arrives and changes the necessary outcomes.

When the economic buyer changes, assume that the client's signals are similar, but the outcomes need to change. In addition, assume you will need to discuss the situation and outcomes with the new economic buyer.

Each of these means your economic buyer is now your technical buyer. That's okay. Assuming you still want the work, you now ask the question, "I'd like to verify the outcomes with the economic buyer. Who can say Yes to this proposal?"

Don't wait too long for that information. I don't wait longer than a week. If I still can't get an appointment with the economic buyer, I drop this work. (I remind the person that I write an email newsletter, so I can maintain contact with them.)

Do not pursue work where the client doesn't want you. Stop with this client and find other clients.

Sometimes, there are internal changes that are great for the original buyer, but delay you from starting. Often, that happens when the buyer has a new role.

6.10.2 *Buyer Has a New Role*

Your buyer had a specific role, responsible for the outcomes you outlined in your proposal. When buyers have new roles, they might have fewer, different, or more responsibilities.

But that client probably wants different outcomes.

If the buyer has a new role, consider an abbreviated discovery call where you learn about the buyer's new responsibilities, outcomes, and when the client wants to talk with you again.

If the buyer wants the same outcomes and is still the economic buyer, check to see when you might see the contracting from your proposal.

Whatever you do, wait for a purchase order to start the work.

6.10.3 *"Please Start Anyway"*

Sometimes, you and the client build a ton of rapport. This person agrees to the option in your proposal and your fee—verbally. However, you don't have a PO or a signed contract yet.

The client says, "I know we haven't done the contracting yet, but please start anyway."

However, you don't know the state of the proposal, the contracting, the terms.

Worse, you have no idea how long the client will take to do all the contracting. One of my more memorable clients took a year from the time I offered them the first proposal to when I started the work. In between, we continued to negotiate the number of people in the workshop, the workshop fee, and the terms.

If a client pressures you to start without a purchase order, you can ask, "Where is the proposal in your process?" Then, wait for the answer. Decide if you will proceed anyway. That's your business decision.

However, I have found in the face of a persistent client, I have an easy answer. That sentence is, "No."

If you want to say more, you can say, "I don't start work without a Purchase Order and a deposit, or payment in full."

I strongly recommend you wait to start the work. That's because you can't tell if the organization will change or if your buyer will change—and they need different work, not this work.

If you do start work, you will find yourself working for free.

Sometimes, even if you track the proposal, the client rejects the proposal.

6.11 When the Client Rejects Your Proposal

Clients reject proposals for many reasons. Very few of those reasons have to do with fees.

If you and the client trust and respect each other, consider asking the client to refer you to other potential clients who share the client's challenges.

6.12 **Now Try This for Proposals**

In your consulting notebook, write this down:

1. You might have a different kind of business than I do. What information do you need to create proposals the client will accept?
2. How long do you want to take to write a proposal?
3. Have you seen other proposal problems?
4. When will you decline to work with a client? Write down your needs to work with a client.
5. Will you always wait for a PO to start the work? If not, write down when you will begin the client work.

Now it's time to set a fee for the work you proposed.

CHAPTER 7

Set Reasonable Fees

Many consultants worry that their fees are too high. However, successful independent consultants worry that their fees are too low and do not reflect the value of the work.

However, both the too-high fee and too-low fee can prevent consulting success. So, first, let's start by considering the value of money. For me, money offers freedom.

7.1 Money Creates Freedom

I don't use money to "keep score" against my fellow consultants. I don't know their fees, and I don't care.

Money offers me the freedom to plan for the present and the future.

When consultants make enough money, they can choose:

- Which engagements to take. With enough money, consultants can avoid challenging clients or boring engagements to pay the mortgage.
- When and which learning opportunities to take.
- When and how many vacations to take.

Money is a tool. I am worth—at least—what I charge for fees. I use money as a tool to create a better life, not just for me but for my family, too.

Avoid setting your fees too low or too high. If your fee is too low, you can't make enough money. If your fees are too high, you might have fewer clients. (That extra in-office time might be what you want.)

Instead, learn to value your time and what that time is worth to the client.

Let's start with how you think about the value of your time.

7.2 What's Your Time Worth to You?

Successful independent consultants cannot work every day of every week of every year. Start thinking about how much work you want in a given year.

When I started my business, I wanted two weeks of actual vacation and two weeks of school holidays. In addition, I set aside two weeks to invest in my learning, for a total of six weeks off.

Of the 52 weeks in a year, I was now down to 46 possible weeks of work.

Could I fill those 46 weeks with client work? No, because that's not the kind of practice I wanted. I knew I would work for clients fewer than 46 weeks a year. How much fewer? I conducted informational interviews with local consultants about how they ran their companies.

At that time, Geoff Day, the owner of The Consulting Exchange, helped local companies find consultants. While his firm wasn't right for me, he asked this valuable question:

"What products will you create so you don't have to always exchange time for money?"

Given my work, I knew I needed to invest time in creating my intellectual property in various forms: talks, workshops, articles, books, and more. That would help me create consistent content marketing that would attract potential clients. How much time did I need to spend on intellectual property development each week?

I had no idea. So I reviewed what my different kinds of work weeks looked like:

- Client-only weeks, where I expect to work with a client all week. Even with my preparation, I knew I would not market myself during those weeks.

- A mix of coaching or consulting sessions with clients. I still have time for content marketing those weeks.
- Conference-only weeks still require most of my time, but I can use both content (presentations) and active marketing (networking) during those weeks.
- Vacation weeks, when I don't work.
- Learning weeks, where I take workshops or learn specific areas to increase my value to my clients.
- In-office weeks mean I spend the entire week creating intellectual property and using content marketing to attract clients.

You might not choose to participate in conferences. However, every successful consultant I know takes both vacation and learning time. No one can work all the time and be effective for clients.

Even when I took interim management contract work at the start of my consulting business, I kept a day a week for my marketing. That day allowed me to continue to attract potential clients. Too many consultants fall into the trap of working full-time for one client and letting their marketing slide. But content marketing attracts clients, so successful consultants create continual marketing activities.

This thinking helped me decide how many "weeks" of work I could do in a year. I assumed I could have clients pay me an average of 20 hours for those 46 weeks a year—which translates to 21 weeks a year. So I chose to use the 21 weeks as the middle of a range of work.

Now, based on working between 18-24 weeks a year, what did I want to charge? That was my weekly starting point. What mix of products and services would get me to that amount of money? That's how I set my initial "daily" rate. (I still didn't charge by the hour, but that rate helped me think about how to create project-based rates.)

You might think differently about your time. However, I don't know of a successful consultant who creates a sustainable revenue stream without thinking about their time and what their time is worth. Your time creates the "floor," the least amount of money you will charge for a proposal. Add the client benefits to that floor.

If you see consultants busy all the time and barely making ends meet, their fees are too low.

Consider how you think about the value of your experience and time so you can set reasonable fees and explain your worth to your clients.

Let's discuss how you might set your fees.

7.3 Set Your Fee

I know of three ways to value your time for your clients:

- Hourly rate or time and materials.
- Project-based rates.
- Value-based fees

I don't recommend hourly rates. However, your clients might think of hourly rates first.

7.3.1 Hourly Rates

Companies are familiar with hourly rates. That's how they pay employees and contractors—by the hour. That pay-for-time thinking often colors how companies think about what they pay consultants.

Worse, the large consulting firms charge by the hour. These consulting firms do not charge by the project or by value—they charge their clients for time.

However, charging for time creates a problematic dynamic and can undermine the relationship you built with the client. The consultant wants more hours to make more money. The client wants fewer hours to spend less money.

But hourly fees ignore the idea of the client paying for outcomes, which will improve the client's work. When everyone's talking about hours, no one's talking about results—the value you offer.

In the past, I offered hourly-based coaching for people as an experiment to try me out. Then, if they liked me, we could create a coaching project with outcomes.

I advise against any charging by the hour—for anything. Instead, consider project-based or product-based fees.

7.3.2 *Project-Based Fee*

Consider calling each engagement a project in your proposals. Then, each project has specific start and end dates based on this client's desired outcomes. That allows you to create projects that work for the client and you.

For example, here's how to create a project for a custom workshop. Even though you already know the outcomes the client wants, you might want to iterate on the syllabus with the client.

You can then create a proposal that says, "A customized workshop project, consisting of:

- Up to three calls in advance with you to clarify the customization and learning objectives.
- Three workshop days.
- Remote debrief three business days after the project ends. We'll book the debrief when we book the workshop.

Now the client knows they're not just paying you for the three days of the workshop. You offer much more value.

Even if you've delivered this workshop before, every customization takes time. Instead of trying to estimate, I right-size the project pieces. For example, I chunk each part of the syllabus into 60-90 minute chunks. I have a good idea of how long it takes me to generate that content.

You can do the same.

This way, you don't need to charge the client for the preparation. However, you can build your preparation time into the value the client will receive. Clients who want customization expect to pay a little more.

Now, you know the workshop duration, the number of chunks in the syllabus, and the value your customizations offer the client.

But the real benefit of packaging an engagement as a project lies in any "extra" work I realize I need. During a recent assessment, I asked to speak with two other people—who offered new and different data. When I work as an executive coach or trusted advisor, I can offer another call after the client encounters a particularly challenging situation.

Because I use projects, I don't add extra fees if I realize I need more scope to deliver the outcomes. I can create fair project-based fees when I clarify the boundaries and client outcomes in the discovery call.

Clients don't pay you for your time—they pay you for outcomes. For example, I don't bill for preparation time, coordinating with various people in the organization, or travel time. If you worry about time sinks with the client, specify the client's and your responsibilities in the proposal.

Should you charge for travel? For too long, I carefully tracked my actual travel expenses. I no longer do. I add a reasonable amount for travel into my overall fee. If my client says they need my actual expenses, I include an administration fee, so it's worth it for me to track my actual costs.

As a guideline, if your travel fees dwarf your engagement fees, your fees are too low.

Clients do not choose consultants based on their travel expenses.

The best kind of fees for both the client and the consultant are value-based fees.

7.3.3 *Value-Based Fees*

You have another choice: value-based fees.

Pioneered initially by Alan Weiss in *Million Dollar Consulting: The Professional's Guide to Growing a Practice* WEI16, consultants create value-based fees when they decide on the value of the consulting to the *client* and quote a fee that's a percentage of that client value.

I discussed tangible and intangible benefits in Start with This Proposal Template (p. 89).

Weiss says there are three pieces of value-based fee calculation:

1. Tangible value on an annual basis. To that, add
2. Intangible value times the emotional impact. To that, add
3. Peripheral value from the benefits that help the client avoid future problems, such as layoffs or renegotiating contracts. While these problems appear to be about money, they often involve morale.

All three of these benefits, added together, create value for the client.

Let's imagine the difference between a project-based fee and a value-based fee for a workshop.

The client, Jim, explained they thought they missed at least three million dollars in potential revenue because of late projects. These late projects had at least two causes: how the projects worked and how senior leadership made decisions. In the discovery call, Jim admitted that he worried they also missed another million in recurring service revenue.

Jim estimated the tangible benefits on an annual basis: four million dollars.

Next, the intangible benefits.

On the discovery call, Jim worried that, as a leadership team, they would "never" figure out how to make better decisions. If they couldn't learn what and how to do this work, this role was not worth his time. He didn't want to leave, but he couldn't stay.

That meant that the ineffectiveness of the six-person leadership team hurt the organization and tempted Jim to consider leaving. The entire leadership team was at risk. The value of intangible benefits includes the leadership team salaries plus the cost of hiring a new manager to replace Jim.

While you can search online for "typical" leadership salaries, consider using a conservative estimate. Here, I'm using an average annual salary of $200,000. The cost to replace a manager ranges from one to three times that manager's salary. So a conservative estimate to replace an entire senior leadership team would be six (people) times the $200,000, $1.2 Million.

Finally, the peripheral benefits.

Jim realized that the organization's "randomness" didn't just cost them time and money as per the tangible benefits. The company was losing its most valuable technical people. The most recent three people who'd quit each said, "I can't work in a place where management can't decide which work is most important."

When some senior people leave, the remaining people can take more responsibility. However, if too many people go, morale drops, and more people leave. At some point, only the people who can't find new jobs remain.

That's an indirect cost to the organization. Jim chose peripheral benefits of the cost to replace the five people who'd recently left, another $1 Million.

The benefits total $6.2 Million:

- Tangible benefits: $4 million.
- Intangible benefits: $1.2 million.
- Peripheral benefits: $1 million.

When consultants start to consider all the benefits, they realize they can charge a fairer fee based on the value the client can see. Here's how to evaluate benefits to decide on a project-based or a value-based fee:

- A project-based fee might include workshops, consulting, and coaching for leadership and teams. Use the various tangible and intangible benefits to decide which outcomes you recommend to whom.
- A value-based fee would be some percentage (5 - 10%) of the total monetary value you expect the customer to see. Then, explain who will receive the workshops, consulting, and coaching.

Hourly fees narrow your focus to what the client says they want. Value assessment widens your possibilities and allows you to propose and deliver what the client needs.

However, clients only buy value-based fees when they trust you to deliver what they need. And those clients might need to be at the top of the organizational hierarchy.

7.3.4 *Possible Requirements for Value-Based Fees*

Who can buy a proposal with a value-based fee? That depends on what you're proposing.

For example, my retainer agreements are value-based fees. That's because the client knows I will offer substantial value—because they already trust me to deliver that value. Often, that's because the client already had experience with my consulting or content marketing.

Clients need to feel they can trust you before they will entertain the idea of a value-based fee.

Not all economic buyers can approve a single value-based fee. Most managers have an upper limit to what they can spend. I worked with one middle manager to create a series of workshops and coaching he could afford. We restricted each engagement to $25,000 because that was his upper limit.

Learn what your economic buyer can authorize. Then, show all the value with tangible, intangible, and peripheral benefits. Consider how you create several engagements that deliver that value.

So, clients need to trust you and have the money to spend on you.

As a consultant, you have responsibilities, too. How can you know that your work is worth the money you're asking for?

Consult with yourself. Practice saying your fee out loud, possibly in front of a mirror. Note where you pause. Clarify why you worry about this fee. Use all of your critical thinking skills on you so that you can respect yourself and your client.

Successful consultants use project-based fees. Some successful consultants can also command value-based fees. But I don't know any successful consultants who charge by the hour.

Make sure you charge enough for the value you offer. The clients who don't respect consultants will filter themselves out. But the clients who take the opportunity to work with you at a higher fee? They tend to get better results because they trust you. They see the value of those results and are more likely to change to obtain those results.

Regardless of how you create your fees, ensure you feel good about your fee.

7.4 Make Sure You're Happy With Your Fee

Weinberg coined the Principle of Least Regret in *The Secrets of Consulting: A Guide to Giving and Getting Advice Successfully*WCO14: "Set the price so you don't regret it either way."

I test my fees with this question:

"Will I be happy if I get the business or if I don't?"

I know I've set my fee correctly when I'm happy if I get the work and just as happy if I don't.

Sometimes, you can ask for something other than money. One client tried to pressure me into taking less than what I thought was reasonable for a fee. Instead of just taking a lower fee, I suggested they pay part of my fee in other ways, including a dinner with the executives of their best customer. I had that dinner, which turned into several engagements with their customer. I was happy about getting that business.

Another client said, "We don't pay consultants your fees." I showed them the value. Nope, they didn't pay those fees. I declined to change my fee.

Later, I spoke with a colleague who proposed and attempted that work. He said, "It was terrible. They were the 'Client from Hell.' They didn't respect me *and* they didn't change anything."

That client didn't respect consultants and the value they offered—and that disrespect had nothing to do with the fee. It was a classic case of bullying. If you placated them and took their counteroffer, they didn't respect you for valuing yourself enough. If you stood your ground, they didn't engage with you. They had no idea of mutual benefits. I was thrilled I didn't take that business.

Don't undersell yourself. Use your value and all the potential client value to generate your fees.

7.5 Set Fees for Writing and Speaking

As an inexperienced writer or speaker, you'll write—for "free"—on your blog and in your newsletter. You'll speak for free at professional meetings that don't require travel. I wrote "free" because you can never tell if a potential client will hire you based on your writing. However, no one pays you *directly* for that writing or speaking.

"Free" writing and speaking helps you practice your writing and speaking craft. While these free opportunities expose you to possible clients, exposure doesn't pay your bills.

The more you write and speak, the more likely you'll build your reputation. That's when you'll receive invitations to write and speak outside your local area. (Because writing is about intellectual property, see Write for Others, p. 131, for ways to think about writing compensation.)

Long ago, when I took too many low-paying speaking engagements, Jerry Weinberg recommended I ask this question:

How much is the honorarium?

I have a simple guideline: When other people will make money from my expertise and time, I ask for payment. That includes corporate requests, money-making conferences, and if I have to leave my home office to speak in person.

Be wary of work for exposure, not money. People die of exposure—both hot and cold. When you make enough money from your unique content, you can choose to vacation in a hot or cold place.

Before you agree to write or speak for free, evaluate the opportunity. What will both of you gain?

I always negotiate for a fee when a company contacts me.

7.6 **Negotiate With Companies for Speaking Fees**

Imagine this scenario: A Very Large and Famous Company asks you to speak to their people "just for an hour." They tell you that you won't have to prepare anything. You also will gain a lot of exposure to their managers, who supposedly will buy your consulting.

You might want to say, "Yes!" because you want to work with this client.

Before you say yes, consider asking these questions:

- Who else will be there? (Am I the only speaker?)
- Do you have specific outcomes you want to achieve? (Do they want something custom from you?)
- Are there boundaries on what I can and cannot say? (Do I need to censor my ideas?)

These questions help frame the context while I build trust with the client.

When I ask these questions, I often discover that the client wants me to participate in a panel and at least one or two organizing calls before the event. The larger the client, the more they have expectations about my participation in their pre-talk rituals. That's why I charge them at least a minimum fee representing about a day of the value of my time.

I don't charge for each hour of speaking—that's hourly rates applied to speaking. Instead, I create a project-based fee that offers different client outcomes. Sometimes, I develop a proposal for a speaking engagement.

That proposal is worth my time because I offer more valuable options the client didn't consider yet. Then I can explain the value behind my fees.

Set a fee that reflects the value you bring and receive to and from the client.

7.7 Set a Fee That Reflects Mutual Value and Benefit

If you charge by the hour, you can't make enough money for the value you provide. You might even feel a cash flow pinch while you wait for clients to pay you. Instead, set a fee based on the value you provide.

Use the client's desired outcomes to explain the value you offer.

You don't know what the client can or cannot afford, so when you propose an engagement, associate a fee with each option based on the value the client can expect. Clients can find the money if they perceive your value.

Beware of the client who wants you to take care of them and how they make money. For example, I've worked with several non-profit organizations that said, "We're a non-profit, and we don't have a lot of money."

I said, "Being a non-profit means you don't distribute profit. It has nothing to do with the money you charge for your products and services." If a non-profit said that to you, consider learning about the various forms of corporations.

If you charge your clients less than what you are worth, you're taking care of the client. In exchange, you're not taking care of yourself, and that's a lose-lose proposition for you.

Instead, consider that higher fees might help you meet and work for better clients.

7.8 Use Higher Fees to Get Better Clients

Instead of thinking of a fee as a transaction, think of explaining the outcomes, value, and fee as part of how you build a relationship with this client. In my experience, clients respect consultants who move from a transactional approach to a relationship approach.

That respect sets the tone for a better and longer-term client relationship.

That respect shows in how fast the client responds to a proposal, all the contracting issues, and when you are available to start an engagement.

One of the reasons to get better clients and those higher fees is that you can make enough money in one engagement to maintain reasonable work practices for yourself.

Too many consultants exist in a state of "bad-busy." They're busy all the time on client work. They don't have the time to invest in their content marketing, time to learn, or even take a vacation.

In my experience, those consultants exist in one of these states:

- Their fees are so low that they must take every possible engagement.
- They're afraid to tell a client "No."
- They sell commodity work. They're busy now—and they can't predict when the commodity work will end.

I see many consultants make a reasonable living—by being busy all the time.

However, I want something different from my consulting business—to engage in productive work. That's good-busy. That's why I spend time creating new intellectual property, learning, and working with clients.

If you think you "can't" charge a high-enough fee to offer you some freedom, remember that your first sale is to yourself. Remind yourself of the value you provide and the value the client will receive from your work.

For too long, my fees were too low. Then, I started to describe the value in my proposals. You might discover, as I did, that when I raised my fees, I got better clients.

7.9 Now Try This to Set Your Reasonable Fees

In your consulting notebook:

1. What does money mean to you? If money means something other than freedom, write an essay about the meaning money has for you in your consulting notebook. Then, use that essay to discuss fees with yourself first.
2. If a potential client says, "We'd like you to come in for a day." How will you decide whether to take that engagement? What will you charge?
3. Decide how you want to set your fees. Then, decide when you want to review that decision.
4. Think about a recent situation where you helped a client or part of an organization change. Assess the tangible, intangible, and peripheral benefits of that work. Could you have charged 10% of that value as a fee? Why or why not?

Now that you've considered your fees, it's time to consider the client paperwork and your intellectual property. All those agreements are part of the client relationship.

CHAPTER 8

Manage Your Intellectual Property

As a successful independent consultant, your content marketing attracted a client. The potential client liked what they heard in the discovery call, proposal, and options (with fees) for the engagement.

However, now it's time to complete all the client paperwork, especially the issues of who owns the intellectual property before, during, and after the engagement.

While I am not a lawyer, I hope this chapter helps you consider your options. Always read and research, so you're comfortable with your decisions.

Paperwork that affects your intellectual property might include:

- What you can say or write publicly about the client. For example, can you use your client's name in your marketing materials?
- The owner of any intellectual property you bring to, generate with, and leave with the client.

Let's start with the kind of intellectual property you generate.

8.1 Assess Your Intellectual Property

Continual content marketing helps consultants create a wide variety of intellectual property (IP):

- Freely available IP, such as blog posts and newsletters.
- Nominally fee-based IP, such as books.

- More expensive IP, such as custom workshops, custom articles, or custom speaking engagements—anything where you might leave a "document" with the client.

You own the copyright to all of that work, including your proposals.

However, you can only effectively use all your IP if you read all the contracts a client offers you. Successful independent consultants read all contracts a client offers—every contract, every time.

8.2 Read All Legal Agreements

Even though you already offered a proposal with fees, many clients want you to sign these two legal agreements:

- A Non-Disclosure Agreement (NDA).
- A Statement of Work (SOW) with Terms.

Even though you specified terms in your fees, some clients ignore them. The clients copy and paste their terms into the SOW and expect you to agree to their terms.

As a general guideline, read everything. You might discover the NDA and SOW—together—create one general agreement. That agreement might be different from what you proposed.

As you read through what the client sent you, note anything you don't understand or concerns you. Then ask the relevant people at your client to clarify your concerns.

We'll start with the contract most organizations ask you to sign first: a Non-Disclosure Agreement, the NDA.

8.2.1 Read the NDA

A potential client may ask you to sign an NDA even before starting a discovery call. Those clients worry about protecting their IP, even as they want to explore how you might help them change. The NDA protects everyone's intellectual property—yours and your client's.

Most NDAs discuss the difference between publicly known information and what you might need to learn for your work. Look for paragraphs that discuss:

- The duration of the NDA.
- The intellectual property the NDA covers.
- The industries or competitors the NDA covers.

Many organizations will ask you to sign an NDA that stays in effect for one to three years. While three years might seem like a long time, consider the case where you can work on different client challenges during the NDA duration.

However, be aware of very long NDAs, especially if those NDAs restrict your ability to use that client's name in your marketing materials. One client asked me to sign an NDA that was in effect for ten years, and during that time, I could not mention that I worked with the client.

The ten years duration was excessive. Their lawyers worried that I would talk about them. (The lawyers worried even when I pointed to "case" studies on my site that anonymize my clients.)

Instead, I asked them how long their senior managers' stock options would vest. They said, "Three years." I told them I would happily sign an NDA that was in effect for three years. Longer than that, and I needed to understand more about their business. (I was concerned they were doing something illegal.) Why would they ask me to sign an NDA longer in duration than their managers' vesting?

After the duration, consider who owns what. Many of my clients have experience working with software *contractors* who write code or tests for hire. The client owns the code or tests when the two parties end the contract. When contractors work for hire, they cannot take any of their work with them. Everything stays with the client.

However, your consulting or workshops are not work for hire. Because you build your offerings on your value, you offer custom services that no one else can offer. That means you must retain all rights to your intellectual property—at the start of the engagement, during, and at the end. The client does not own your intellectual property at any time.

One of my clients, Acme, wanted me to sign their "standard" NDA for a short workshop. However, they did not understand I was a consultant, not a contractor.

Know Your Status: Contractor or Consultant

In the United States, taxes apply differently to contractors vs. consultants. Consultants choose their clients and tend to work for several clients during the year. And consultants enter into a client relationship directly with the client.

Many contractors work with one client for months or years at a time. Because of tax law, these contractors look a lot like employees. That creates tax liability for the client. That's why US companies avoid hiring contractors directly. Instead, these companies use agencies as a middle-person to hire the contractor. The agency employs the contractor—not the client.

Agencies sign NDAs with clients all the time. If you choose to work for an agency, learn what the blanket NDA says about your IP. Many US companies try to own *all* of their employees' or contractors' IP, including poetry or fiction writing.

If you work through an agency, learn what the NDA covers, especially if you create content.

Because Acme had only worked with contractors, their standard NDA said that they owned my workshop at the end of it. I objected to that and asked to speak with their lawyer. After an hour-long conversation, we finally agreed on a fair NDA.

If I can't dissuade clients from owning my IP at the end of an engagement, I decline this work. We don't have a mutually beneficial relationship.

Contracting and consulting are both honorable work. However, know the role you choose. If an agency represents you, you are a contractor.

If you are a contractor, it's possible that whatever you create *while* you work at the client *does* belong to the client. It doesn't matter if you develop scripts to monitor their security or write code to parse an input string. You can't take that code with you when you leave. Worse, depending on the NDA, they might own any other work you create, such as fiction, nonfiction, or music. It all depends on the contract they ask you to sign.

You can always ask for exclusions for their standard NDA.

But the NDA is only the first legal agreement you need to sign. Sometimes, the client also wants you to sign a non-compete agreement. Before you even look at that agreement, search to see if your state (or country) allows non-competes.

8.2.2 *Beware of Non-Compete Clauses*

Non-compete clauses bar people from taking future jobs in a specific industry. For example, some hospitals have non-compete agreements for certain kinds of physicians. However, more non-competes are not enforceable. Search online to see which non-compete agreements remain enforceable.

Some of my clients have wanted me to sign an NDA that included a non-compete—I couldn't work in their industry for five years or more. I explained I would negotiate that point. If they paid me a reasonable, hefty fee for those five years, I would be happy to look for clients outside their industry. But, because they didn't want to pay me that hefty fee, they crossed that line out.

Here are my NDA guidelines:

1. Read the entire agreement. I often print it to note where I have questions and concerns.
2. Realize the entire agreement is the agreement. If you question something or anyone changes anything, reread the whole agreement. For example, paragraph 3 changes might affect the meaning of paragraph 7.
3. Watch for "typical" NDAs that assume you are a contractor. You deserve your *consulting* NDA.
4. Watch for agreement terms that last longer than three years.
5. Watch for industry non-competes or exclusions. For example, "Consultant agrees to not work in travel or entertainment for x years."
6. If you need a lawyer to sign an NDA, either negotiate *much* more money or decline the work. Lawyers cost much more money than you can imagine.

Contracts can reinforce a beneficial client-consultant relationship. However, too many of my clients start with contracts that assume I am not trustworthy. I find it humorous that a large Fortune 100 client wants me to indemnify them if something goes wrong. That's why I have errors and omissions insurance.

I'm not willing to spend the money on a lawyer to review contracts. I don't work with clients like that.

Create guidelines that work for you. An NDA is supposed to protect the client *and* you. Ensure you don't sign your intellectual property to a client without realizing you've done so.

The next agreement might be the Statement of Work, the SOW.

8.2.3 *Read or Generate the SOW*

I write proposals that look like a Statement of Work (SOW). And sometimes, the client either restates my proposal in their form. Or they ask me to generate an SOW.

The SOW is your last chance to write down the payment terms you want for your fee. For example, you might want a deposit or payment in full for short-term engagements. Or, you can offer a discount for payment in full two weeks before the engagement starts. The SOW is your last chance to clarify the payment terms.

Even when I explain my payment terms in my proposals, somehow, by magic, the client changes those terms in the SOW. Read the entire SOW to get the correct terms.

Even if you get the SOW right, you might still have a client whose Accounts Payable staff thinks their job includes negotiation with you.

I start with the economic buyer. I write to explain why I must decline that PO and express my regret that we couldn't work together at the original fee for the original terms.

If I still want the business, I inform the economic buyer that I can take those terms, but at a much higher fee. (That fee is often peanuts to the client but makes a huge difference for my cash flow.)

Only the economic buyer can fix the process that requires you to take their terms instead of yours.

Now that we've addressed the most common contracts with corporate clients, it's time to discuss other contracts. You will sign an agreement about your IP if you write or speak for webinars, conferences, or companies.

8.3 Understand Your IP Rights

Intellectual property is property, and it has value. Companies love IP because they can depreciate it, adding to their bottom line. (If you want to do that, talk to a lawyer and an accountant.)

Every piece of your intellectual property is real property with real value—because you own the copyright to that information.

Unless and *until* you sign a contract giving away your copyright, you own the copyright to that information.

Because you own the copyright, you can exploit that copyright in many ways:

- Repurpose your writing into presentations or a book—and vice versa.

- Change the form of the IP, changing from text, print, audio, video, and back again.
- You can decide which forms to offer in which territories worldwide—for free or for money.

Dean Wesley Smith, the fiction writer, calls this a *Magic Bakery*. (See *The Magic Bakery* SMI17 for more details, specifically about fiction.) Because nonfiction writers create IP, the Magic Bakery applies to consultants, too.

You can only exploit all these rights if you own the copyright. Once you sign away your copyright, the person or company who owns the copyright can decide how to use your material. For example, they can create workshops, ebooks, audio, and print books from your IP. (Yes, this is a risk for any work-for-hire writing.)

Would they do this? Sometimes. I was surprised when a magazine published some of my columns. After I received the book, I reviewed the contract, and yes, they had the IP rights to do this. The risk of my magazine columns in a book was a small price to pay for my name to appear next to more famous people monthly.

If you sign away your copyright, the copyright owner can create "derivative" work that you might not recognize. And the owner can put your name on that derivative work: "from the book foo by *your name*," where foo is the name of the book to which they own the copyright.

The copyright owner has all the power. Even if you created the original version of the work, if you sign away your copyright, you don't have to approve or agree to anything.

Worse, once you relinquish your copyright, you cannot legally reuse that material. If you wrote a blog post and you sold the copyright to that post, you cannot reuse the words as you wrote them originally. That's because copyright covers the form of the *creation*. I recommend you buy a copy of *The Copyright Handbook: What Every Writer Needs to Know* FIS17. That book will answer all your questions and help you solve problems you might encounter.

Remember this idea:

When you create content, you can exploit it to make more money.

Intellectual property can help you create more income streams, which supports a successful consultant's business model.

Part of that business model is to decide when to write or speak for others and what those others can do with your IP.

8.3.1 *Write for Others*

In Write to Share Your Unique Expertise (p. 34), I suggested you consider many venues for your writing.

When you write for your site, you own the copyright. Consider when to write for other sites, especially if you want to showcase your expertise widely.

You have several options for how to write for other sites.

Sometimes, those sites repost my content—with my permission. I own the copyright, so they need to ask permission. Depending on the circumstances, I decide whether to charge them a fee to use my material.

Sometimes, I write unique content for another site, both for first-publication rights and as work-for-hire.

When clients want first-publication rights, they pay me a fee for the exclusive use of that content for some relatively short time, often 30 days. After that time is up, I have the right to repost the article on my site.

My work-for-hire is also original content. However, I ask for a larger fee because I no longer own the copyright. Some of those sites don't want me to repost the article on my site. Read any contract carefully to see what they will give you in return.

When writing for other sites, negotiate your compensation to include a short bio with a link to your site. That bio is an example of mutual benefit. The client receives original content, and curious readers can see what else you might do.

Decide if and how you want to write for others and what you want for that writing.

Remember, the content creator always owns the copyright unless that creator signs a contract.

If you write a book, I recommend you keep your copyright.

If you choose to speak at conferences and for companies, make sure you have a contract for that, too.

8.3.2 *Speak for Others*

I suggested you speak widely in Speak to Establish Your Expertise (p. 36). Some of those venues will want to record your talk. I decide what to do based on the availability of the video:

- When all the videos freely and readily available, I do not ask for an extra fee.
- If conferences put my talks behind a paywall, I ask for a higher fee. The conference will continue to make money from my content—I should gain some benefit, also.
- When clients keep my recording for exclusive use, I ask for a higher fee.

Clarify what the conference or client will do in advance of any recording.

Years ago, I discovered some clients used a previously recorded webinar as an information product that they sold online. They did not pay me, and they violated our agreement. After a short conversation, they took down the information product.

One client wanted me to teach a workshop once and record it. They thought they could use it again without my instruction or facilitation. However, that's a licensing agreement. Since they didn't want to pay me to license my IP, I declined their kind offer.

However, licensing makes sense for some IP.

8.4 **License Your IP**

Some clients or fellow consultants might want to license your intellectual property, such as a workshop. Here are issues to consider:

- The duration of the license and whether there was an option to renew. (For example, a yearly license renewable at the same or new rate.)
- How much material they could add or change and still call it your work.
- What to do if you, as the creator, wanted to add new material.
- If it's a workshop, the enrollment for one workshop. I always limit the number of people in a workshop because I need to create an environment where all the participants can learn.
- How they will pay you for the license: a per-person charge per class, a yearly flat fee, something else.
- How to evaluate the trainer's capabilities.

You might have other concerns. However, if someone wants to license your IP, consider these questions—especially the duration.

One of my clients wanted to license my class because I limit the number of participants every time. They thought it would be "too expensive" for me to continue to train about 20 people at a time. Then, once we started discussing how I create and run workshops and the necessary license components, they realized I offered them a bargain.

Licensing your IP isn't for everyone. However, it might work for you. Consider researching how other consultants license their IP.

8.5 **Review to Repurpose Your Content**

Review your IP regularly to review your brand and repurpose or exploit your content. You can only repurpose your content if you retain your copyright.

Consider these options for your IP:

- A Q&A (Question and Answer) book, video, or podcast based on what people have asked in your workshops.
- A FAQ (Frequently Asked Questions) post for your site.
- Smaller books that collect various articles and blog posts about one specific topic. Many people like small, focused nonfiction books.

Consider a yearly or more frequent cadence of review.

Your content marketing is your brand, so understand what you offer. Sometimes, my clients and colleagues recognize my value before I do. That's why regular content reviews can help you visualize your value.

When you take the time to review your content, you might realize you write or speak about work you no longer want to perform. That review time is an excellent opportunity to decide what to keep and remove from your consulting offerings.

8.6 Now Try This to Manage Your IP

In your consulting notebook, write the answers to these questions now:

Part 1: Evaluate any contracts you have now.

- If you're still an employee, review all the contracts you signed with your current employer. If your employer owns your non-work IP, consider asking them to remove that part of your contract. Then, you can start to write and speak without violating your employment agreement.
- If you're a consultant, review all your current client contracts, including any writing and speaking contracts. Are you happy with them? If you made a mistake and cannot renegotiate, chalk that up to experience. Now, decide how you will avoid making the same mistake again.

If you still need to start your content marketing, start that and return to this section in 30-60 days.

Part 2: Assess your IP and write down the answers in your consulting notebook:

1. How many blog posts, articles, and newsletters share a common theme? How else can you repurpose that content? For example, I only realized I had written many articles on estimation when I looked. So I organized those articles into a book.
2. What else do people ask you to offer? Have you written blog posts, articles, or newsletters about those topics? If not, brainstorm several possibilities and decide if you want to write or speak and where.

Now that you've completed all the contracting, it's time to deliver the engagement. The engagement allows you to strengthen relationships across the client organization.

CHAPTER 9

Strengthen the Client Relationship

Successful independent consultants have all kinds of stories about engagements gone bad. That's why many successful consultants recognize incongruence in the consultant-client relationship and manage those relationships.

When client relationships remain based on mutual trust and respect, consultants can offer options to clients, especially as the consultant learns and adapts to the client's current state.

Here's how to know you have a client relationship based on mutual trust and respect:

- The client is willing to discuss their concerns with your advice, not dismiss that advice.
- You can bring your concerns to the client as you discover new information.
- The client will engage with you again or refer others to you.

However, not all engagements go well. And that's when strengthening the client relationship matters the most. Even if you have a "Client from Hell," you can still manage yourself to offer the benefit of the engagement to the client.

First, let's start with congruence for mutual trust and respect.

9.1 Create Congruent Relationships

Congruence is a way to find the balance between you and your needs, the other person and their needs, and the entire context. I first read about congruence in *Software Quality Management, Vol 2: First-Order Measurement* WEI93.

Any of four incongruent stances can kill a successful engagement: blaming, placating, super reasonable, and irrelevant.

When we don't take the other person into account, we blame them. I've met too many consultants who blame their clients for failing to follow the consultant's advice, even though the client's system might prevent them from doing so.

If you ignore yourself and your needs, you might placate or appease other people. People pleasers often placate others. If you tend to be people-pleasing, stay aware of the engagement you agreed to with the economic buyer—and avoid adding anything extra.

Super reasonable people forget about the humans in the organization. Instead, they only think about the context of the situation. But consulting is a relationship business. So when consultants ignore everyone's feelings—including their own—they don't serve the client that well.

When people take an irrelevant stance, they ignore all three: themselves, the other, and the context. I've seen consultants who offer a "standard" product or service. One notable consultant always assumed his tool would automate whatever the client needed for automation. However, after several years, his clients' context changed, and no one needed his tool. He became irrelevant because he did not think of the people in the situation.

That's the brief idea behind congruence. When we balance ourselves with the other and the context, we can create a relationship of mutual trust and respect. That's what successful independent consultants do with each client.

Congruent behavior helps you find your courage and self-esteem so you can do your best work and create the outcomes everyone expects. Revisit your Relationship-Building or Influencing Skills (p. 6) every so often and see how you've evolved.

Remember that clients are people with challenging problems. Those problems offer consultants a chance to serve their clients and support the clients' changes—as long as the consultant remains congruent.

9.2 Review Your Congruent Behaviors

As part of your engagement, you might see situations you did not expect. Your client, the economic buyer, needs more information. Successful consultants remain congruent and offer their clients that information.

Here is unexpected information I've offered my clients in the past:

- Report bad news that no client would want to hear.
- Recognize that the engagement's planned interventions were insufficient for the client to change.
- Even though the economic buyer created this engagement, the people at the client do not want the changes. (The buyer inflicted my help.)

Let's start with reporting bad news in a congruent way.

9.2.1 *Report Bad News*

Jim, a new senior manager, wanted an assessment of why the projects were all so late. We agreed that I would do an assessment and present the results. As part of the engagement, we made a list of all the people I needed to interview.

But, the people I needed to see wouldn't accept my meeting requests. Finally, during our eventual meetings, I asked why scheduling appointments was so tricky.

One of the managers said, "We're all looking for new jobs. We don't trust our management to keep us on and create a place where we want to work."

I asked if I could inform Jim that the managers were looking for new jobs.

The manager said no, he wanted to remain anonymous. I verified that several other managers felt the same way and that they wanted to be anonymous.

After my appointments that day, I spoke with Jim. I said, "Several of your managers appear to be looking for new jobs. Do you want to retain them?"

He nodded and said, "Yes, I do. Which people?"

"I'm not able to tell you who. But several."

He nodded and said, "I just don't know what to do."

"Would you like some suggestions?" I asked.

We discussed several of his options. He took my advice and managed to retain most of the management staff. While I did not expand the scope of this engagement, Jim and I discussed his immediate options.

That's a form of bad news.

Sometimes, the bad news takes a different form, where the client's system or culture means the client cannot change.

9.2.2 *The Client Can't Change*

During an engagement, you deliver the work you agreed upon with the client. However, the client's culture prevents the specific changes the economic buyer wants.

When I realize this, I gather qualitative and quantitative data. I anonymize the qualitative data because I'm not about to blame people for optimizing their work in my client's environment. I also anonymize the quantitative data.

You have several choices:

- When do you want to explain the challenges to your client? I often gather enough data and then present the data as early as possible.
- Do you want to stop this engagement? I have yet to stop an engagement, but I deliver relatively short engagements unless it's Trusted Advisor work.

- Do you want to propose different work to solve the environment or culture problems at the client? If so, that's much more valuable work, and that extra value requires higher fees.

In my experience, economic buyers don't like surprises. Recognize how you can explain the challenges as early as possible. In addition, explain what you can do in this engagement to support your client's changes.

However, sometimes, the client does not want to change.

9.2.3 *The Client Doesn't Want to Change*

As you work during the engagement, you've offered the client several options for what and how to change. However, the client rejects all those possibilities.

I don't worry when clients reject my suggestions. However, I worry when they don't want to pay me for the engagement because they can't change.

What do you do then?

Long ago, I taught a workshop. The economic buyer had agreed that my suggestion would "shake things up" there. Part of how I shook things up was by trusting people to do their jobs.

The client's management refused to consider trusting the people in the organization.

After the workshop, the economic buyer told me they could not implement my suggestions. Therefore, while they had paid me the deposit (half the fee), they wouldn't pay me the remainder for the engagement.

I reminded them of these items from the proposal:

- The benefits they wanted from the workshop regarding faster work and more cross-training in the teams.
- The delays and costs they currently had.
- I asked them if they still wanted those benefits. My economic buyer said, "But we, as managers, have to change. We don't want to."

I said, "You could hire me to help you see the benefits of changing your management."

The client said, "No."

I did ask for and received the rest of my payment because I had a Purchase Order. Many companies treat POs as contracts. If I had started work without a PO, I would not have had any recourse.

That client never hired me again. However, several people in that workshop hired me later when they became managers.

Consultants can offer recommendations or support for the client's changes. We can't make our clients change.

The longer you work, the more chances you have to practice being congruent—even in difficult conversations.

That's why consultants need to recognize their incongruent behaviors.

9.3 Recognize Our Incongruent Behaviors

Perfect congruence is impossible because we are human. However, with practice, we can see our incongruent patterns. I prefer to see these patterns as traps.

I've seen these incongruent traps:

- When the client does something against your advice, you might want to tell them they're wrong.
- You want to add more work to the engagement because the client needs those outcomes.
- During the engagement, you realize you're working at the wrong level, and you start to consult with people who did not hire you.

Here's how these traps work, starting with the client doing something "wrong."

9.3.1 *Trap: The Client Does It "Wrong"*

Sometimes, you offer an engagement, such as a workshop, where the client is supposed to follow your advice to the letter.

Fred, an agile coach, told the client they could get more work done in much less time if they adopted his specific agile approach. The client was thrilled with the outcomes Fred promised and engaged Fred to teach workshops and coach the teams after the workshops.

Fred taught two teams in one workshop and started coaching. However, the teams could not sustain working the way Fred taught them because of their environment.

Fred blamed the teams for not following his advice.

Fred told the next workshop participants that they had to follow Fred's advice to the letter. The participants could not create their own unique agile approach—they must follow what Fred taught them.

One of the managers in that workshop asked why they couldn't change anything. Fred said, "Because you won't do it right then. You won't get the results I promised."

Fred was correct in a narrow way. If this client *could* have taken his advice, they would be much better off. However, if we assume clients are capable adults, something in their environment prevents them from taking your advice.

Consider how you can See the System that Creates These Pains. If seeing the system is in the scope of your current engagement, do that first and explain what you see to the client. Alternatively, consider asking the client to stop your current engagement and create a new engagement to work on the system instead. Or, you might need to Report Bad News (p. 139).

However, do not add more work to this engagement.

9.3.2 *Trap: You Want to Add More Work*

You see a problem outside the scope of your engagement. And you like this client. You know you shouldn't work for free—but the possibility tempts you. Besides, they need you to do this work.

If you add more work without compensation, you're placating the client and taking care of them. You might not think that's so bad. However, here's what I've found when I see consultants take care of their clients:

- The consultant loses out on more revenue.
- The client loses respect for the consultant and frequently asks for additional free work.
- Too often, the economic buyer and the consultant lose respect for each other.

Should you ever take care of a client? Absolutely, inside the scope of this engagement. Should you ever work for free? I don't think of these services as billable, but here's what I've done with clients:

- Informal, timeboxed meetings with senior managers to scope new engagement possibilities. These meetings act as discovery calls.
- Breakfast or lunch with senior managers to see what their concerns are. A meeting earlier in the day helps use the day's pressure to get to the issues faster. These meetings also act like discovery calls.

I offer nothing over and above the current engagement except for informal conversations.

Your clients are adults. Treat them that way. They will also treat you as an adult businessperson.

9.3.3 *Trap: You Try to Work at a Different Level*

Several years ago, a client asked me to run several agile project workshops. We decided on one workshop to start and see if they liked it.

They did, so we created a six-workshop engagement. I delivered the first two workshops. At the third workshop, several people were hostile. At the first break, one participant said, "I can't believe you're here, telling us everything is optional instead of mandatory."

I'm sure I said something as articulate as, "Huh?"

"We just got the memo that we need to work the way you're teaching us. All of us. All the time. Even if it doesn't work for our team."

I said, "Okay, thanks for telling me."

I sent an email to my contact, the economic buyer. When the class resumed, I addressed this problem and suggested several alternatives to make their lives easier. During our lunch break, I spoke with the economic buyer.

I explained he had diminished my ability to teach with his actions. And that standardizing how people worked wouldn't create an agile environment. If he wanted an agile environment, I needed to work at a different level in the organization.

Every organization has its system of work. Before I taught another workshop, I wanted to consult with my client for a few days. I wanted to explore his system and discuss what happens when management mandates specific ways of working.

He hemmed and hawed for a while. I told him I would not teach another workshop until we met. And the meeting was over and above the workshop fees because I wanted specific leaders there.

It took a couple of weeks, but they did decide to have me in for a couple of days of consulting. That's when I worked with management on their actions.

I see this a lot in my coaching, too. The client asks me for help with specific challenges. And the system of work causes many of those challenges. The client might not be able to address those problems. However, you see the need to work at a variety of levels.

Never offer extra consulting work for free. However, consider adding that work to your current engagement for a fee.

Sometimes, the buyer works in an organization that creates incongruence. Successful independent consultants learn to recognize those traps.

9.4 Recognize Incongruent Client Behaviors

When clients are incongruent, they might appear as the "Client from Hell." Instead of assuming they're hellish, consider possible incongruent behaviors. Here are some of the most common behaviors I've seen:

- The economic buyer is part of a larger group of people with diverse goals
- Change the engagement underway.
- Some people at the client want your help solving their interpersonal problems. But they want you to take responsibility by triangulating the situation rather than helping them learn to solve their problems.

Before you move into problem-solving, review your previous client interactions. Did you have trouble with the proposal or contracting part of the engagement? If so, did some of those problems follow you into the engagement?

9.4.1 *Trap: Conflicting Client Goals*

You and the economic buyer agreed on the goals and benefits of this engagement. However, during the engagement, you realize others do *not* share the goals for this engagement. If those people are senior to your economic buyer, you might have a big problem.

You think you're working toward Outcome A. The other people want you to work toward Outcome B.

Worse, if your economic buyer's peers have opposing goals, you might not achieve what you expected. They might actively work against you.

Several years ago, I assessed a large division of a company. The economic buyer—a very senior manager—wanted to see the reality of the work in his division. The various division managers wanted to keep the facts private.

Was I "caught" in the middle? Only partially. That's because I knew who my client was—the senior manager. I had to build trust and respect with the division managers who did not want to share. I showed them how they would benefit from exposing their data anonymously.

However, I've also been in situations where I had to consider who the client was.

In another assessment, the technical buyer, Ted, introduced me to the economic buyer, Evan. Ted thought everything he did was perfect. However, partway through the first week, I realized Ted had created some of the client's problems. What should I do?

I had several conversations that week with Ted so he could see alternatives. Then, I spoke with Evan and explained that the system Evan and his peers created made it impossible for Ted and his peers to succeed. Instead of looking to blame anyone, I showed them the system.

So far, my assumptions that the economic buyer is the client have worked for me.

That's why I clarify all the outcomes and benefits in the proposal. I want the outcomes and benefits to guide the engagement.

If you see conflicting goals, check with your economic buyer. Verify that no one has changed the desired outcomes.

Sometimes, the economic buyer wants to change the engagement. That's a different problem.

9.4.2 Trap: Change the Engagement Underway

I see two kinds of change: where the client wants you to add more work for the same amount of money and where they want to change the engagement once you start.

You're already delivering value in this engagement. Based on your work, some people have already changed. One of them—maybe even the economic buyer— wants you to do more work in *this* engagement. More work than you proposed. For the same amount of money.

You're flattered. The client perceives so much value they want you to do more!

Think about what they're asking you. The client is asking you to do more work for less money.

You can say, "No, that's out of our agreed-upon scope. If you'd like to re-examine the proposal and if I have the time, we can extend this engagement and my fee."

Only say that if you want to extend the engagement. You might not.

In my experience, they do this with the employees, too. They set the goal. Once the work is underway, they change the objective.

If you think this occurs at your client, go a little "meta" about the engagement—review the client's environment:

- Do employees feel the desired result—their objective—changes as they work?
- Do you see or hear grumbling about feeling as if they can't finish?

You might see other data that tells you this client changes the objective before people finish. If so, here's my advice:

1. Make sure the client knows the boundaries of your work. Refer back to the proposal.
2. Maintain those boundaries yourself. Otherwise, you might fall into the trap of You Want to Add More Work.
3. Consider asking for another engagement to address the client's shifting objectives.

Avoid any changes to the scope of work in the middle of an engagement. If you feel you must, consider how you will explore new objectives with the client, as in Learn with a Discovery Call (p. 78).

What if someone other than the economic buyer asks you to change or do more work? You can politely say, "No, that's out of scope of this engagement."

Don't placate the client and deliver more work for the same money. That's not a congruent approach to mutual trust, respect, or benefits.

I've encountered too many organizations where people don't feel safe when they offer feedback to each other. They want to use the consultant to offer that feedback. That has a name: triangulation.

9.5 Trap: Triangulate Interpersonal Issues

Part of consulting is your ability to offer bad news to the economic buyer. But let's imagine a different scenario. Peter and Paul have trouble communicating with each other. One of them—or worse, both of them— asks you to bring a message to the other person.

They want you to solve their problems without them learning how to do so. That's triangulation.

Triangulation differs from the situation where you need to bring the economic buyer bad news. Nor is it where people with much less organizational power ask you to convey information to management.

Most consultants do manage those situations regularly. Stay congruent and improve your client's trust and respect for you.

In the case of "tell management for me..." ask the requesters to decide if you can use their names or if they feel better if they remain anonymous.

I relay all this possible information:

- Anything about the project, process, or governance data.
- If people appear to be doing a great job and no one in management recognizes their accomplishments.
- If people want a different role.

Triangulation is different.

Sometimes, a manager wants *me* to offer feedback to someone they perceive is failing in their role. Max, a manager, wanted me to explain to Jane that she had done her job wrong. However, reviewing Jane's role was not a part of my engagement.

Instead, I offered to support Max in learning how to provide Jane feedback and maintain psychological safety.

Even if a person wants to offer a manager difficult feedback, I don't triangulate. Instead, I support people learning how to provide feedback.

I only bring the data I see to my clients. If I don't see the data, I don't offer information.

Sometimes, the client no longer fits *your* business model.

9.6 Recognize When This Client No Longer Fits

Let's assume you worked with this client on several successful engagements, strengthening relationships across the organization.

Now, you realize this client no longer fits you and your work. Consider "firing" the client under these circumstances:

- You updated your fees
- You could not do more with this client at this level of the organization.

Let's start with changing fees.

9.6.1 *You Updated Your Fees*

You use project-based fees, but you last changed them a few years ago. Now, you realize it's time to charge more.

You can say something like this: "I've worked with you for x years at this fee. I'm changing my fees to y for my work with you. I would love to retain you as a client. Will my new fee work for you?

If the client says, "No," you say, "I've enjoyed working with you. This engagement will be the last for us." Then, you Ask for a Referral

(p. 152) for new clients. Consider supporting your client when you Refer Other Consultants (p. 214).

What if the client wants to negotiate your fee? You might say, "I'm happy to discuss the outcomes you want." Once you decide on a fee, only negotiate your fee down if you also reduce the expected outcomes. Stick with your new fees. Most independent consultants need to charge more.

However, that conversation might be easier than working with a client who isn't a good fit for you, especially if you no longer want to do this kind of work.

9.6.2 *You No Longer Want to Do This Work*

Part of your proposal was a clause like this: "We can mutually decide to renew this engagement at the current terms" at a given time, such as every quarter. (If you choose a renewable engagement, such as a trusted advisor engagement, put a time limit on it. That limit will allow you to reassess your value and modify your fee.)

Your first quarter's work was terrific. You and the client both profited from your work.

Then, something changed. The second quarter wasn't so much fun. And now the client wants you to stay for the third quarter. Should you? If you take this work, even if you don't like it, can you succeed?

Consider evaluating the mutual benefits you and the economic buyer expect from this engagement. Have any of the benefits or values changed since that first quarter? Remember, as soon as you fulfill the first quarter's engagement, you do not have to renew this engagement. It might be time to renegotiate the agreement.

There is one circumstance in which I will (un)happily fire a client. I fire clients if they don't pay me according to our agreed-upon terms. One client, Acme, managed to pay me according to our terms for the first quarter of a Trusted Advisor engagement. However, Accounts

Payable, AP, didn't pay me according to our terms for the second quarter. I had to get my client involved.

When AP struggled to pay me for the third quarter, I explained to my client that he could fix the payment problem, or I could stop working with him.

Life is too short to work with people who don't appreciate you.

9.6.3 *Fire the Client with Tact*

If you fire a client, use as much tact as possible. Resist screaming and carrying on. You can never tell when the client will refer other people to you.

Long ago, I fired a client because they stopped paying me. I finally received the last bit of money from them almost six months after finishing the work. (I never finished the engagement.)

Three months after their last payment, they referred another client to me. We had a long and productive consulting relationship. The new client said, "I hired you because you're not a pushover."

Surprised me.

9.7 Ask for a Referral

When consultants find great clients, they want to work with those clients again and again on different problems.

Even if you encountered surprises in this engagement, I recommend you ask all the buyers for a referral. Ask the economic buyer because you delivered the outcomes that person wanted. However, ask the other buyers—the technical, coach, and user buyers—for referrals, also.

Here's how I ask:

- I remind the client of the outcomes.
- If the company is large, I ask, "Do you know of anyone else here who could use my services?"

- Regardless of the company size, I ask, "Do you know of a colleague you can refer to me?"

I'm much farther ahead if my client can make that introductory call for me.

You might also ask for a testimonial. I ask for testimonials when I finish an engagement. Sometimes, I ask when I follow up after the engagement.

9.8 Follow Up to Check on Progress

Consider asking for a follow-up call a short time after the engagement. If the client has questions, you'll hear them then. Do offer a few minutes of discussion if they have questions. I often discover my client has done something remarkable. They integrated my recommendations or adapted them and made those ideas their own.

Sometimes, the client realizes they have all new problems. That's terrific because you can ask if they want you to create a new engagement.

9.9 Now Do This to Strengthen Your Client Relationships

These ideas are about building a respectful and trustful relationship with your clients. That's how you'll strengthen that ongoing client relationship.

If you haven't consulted yet, answer these questions thinking about a more senior person in your organization. If you are a consultant, consider your most recent three clients. Then, in your consulting notebook, write down these questions and your answers:

1. When have you realized you behaved incongruently? What did you do to get the relationship back on track?
2. When have you seen your clients behave incongruently? How have you addressed that?

3. Think back to a recent time you wanted to influence someone to change. How attached were you to your solution or answer? How did you explore other possibilities?
4. When have you been pleasantly surprised when you considered new options? When have you been unpleasantly surprised?

This chapter completes how you build your consulting engine. Now it's time to consider the business part of consulting.

PART 2

Create and Maintain a Business That Works for You

Successful independent consultants have two big jobs: they work *in* the business and *on* the business.

Everything you do for your consulting engine is "in" the business. Independent consultants do all the work to acquire and deliver value to clients. If you're like me, that's where you prefer to spend your energy.

Then, there's the part about working "on" the business. We can't only spend our time developing our content for our marketing, writing proposals, and delivering client outcomes—we also need to pay our taxes, maintain our health, and reflect on what's working and what's not working in our business.

Successful independent consultants find ways to work both in and on the business. I recommend you use systems to help you find your balance between the "in" and the "on." That's how you can help your clients—and your business—thrive.

CHAPTER 10
Decide How You Will Make Money

By now, you understand how your content marketing defines your brand and allows and encourages you to integrate your consulting with your marketing. If you're already speaking and writing, conference organizers might ask you to speak. And publishers might ask you to write.

That's all great. However, even when people ask you to speak or write, very few consultants make enough money that way to sustain their businesses. Successful independent consultants choose which products and services to offer and how. That's how they make enough money to create and maintain a thriving business.

Let's start with how you can think about which products and services you might consider and how they apply to your business model.

10.1 Organize Your Products and Services

Most consultants offer these kinds of products and services, modified to meet their ideal client's needs:

- Assessments to see the client's current state.
- Workshops to teach the client a new state.
- Facilitation or consulting about how to support a team or person's changes.
- Coaching to support how people might see how to change over time.
- Advisorship, in some way, to support a client's thinking and changes.

That's why your value and perspective allow you to pick and choose which services to offer and when.

In addition, most consultants can work with clients in-person and remotely.

The difference between consultants who barely make a living and those with thriving businesses is this: successful consultants choose a business model that generates enough revenue to match what they want from their lives.

That's why there are two axes in your business model: Your expertise and the various ways you deliver that expertise. The more ways you can provide your expertise, the more income streams you create.

The Business Model axes show how you can think about which ways to deliver your expertise to potential and current clients.

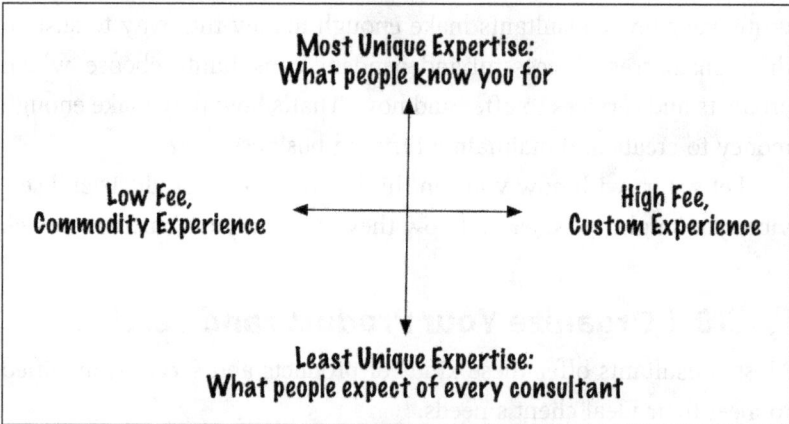

Figure 10.1: Business Model Axes

For example, conference talks or workshops are low-fee. If you offer a "standard" certification workshop at a conference, that would be a low fee and the least unique expertise. On its face, that workshop does not differentiate you from any other consultant.

However, if you have a slightly different perspective on the various problems you want to solve with your clients, you can create a unique conference talk or workshop. While still a low-fee, it's higher on the unique expertise scale.

Your business model depends on your unique value and perspectives.

If your perspective *appears* to be the same as all the other consultants you meet, your content marketing will have to do much more work for you. That's because your clients see your offering as all on the left side of the Business Model Axes.

You might have already built a reputation as a dynamic speaker or effective workshop facilitator. However, if your expertise *appears* to be more of a commodity and less unique, you will have trouble selling anything on the right side of these axes. Even if you think your custom work is worth every penny.

Instead, when you focus on your unique perspective, you can make low-fee conference talks work for your business. That's because those conference talks invite people into your content marketing, where you can then build trust with them.

Successful independent consultants offer enough low-fee experiences to help clients discover them. Then, these consultants offer enough high-fee experiences that the consultant can make money.

Here's what that means for possible income streams.

10.2 Create Multiple Income Streams for Resilience

In Chapter 3, Attract Clients with Content Marketing (p. 27), I suggested that you write and speak to discover and connect with clients through your content marketing.

This Figure 10.2, Possible Business Model on p. 160 applies some of your possible public and private offerings to the business model axes:

Starting from the lower left quadrant, you might offer general conference talks or certification classes. Depending on the clients you

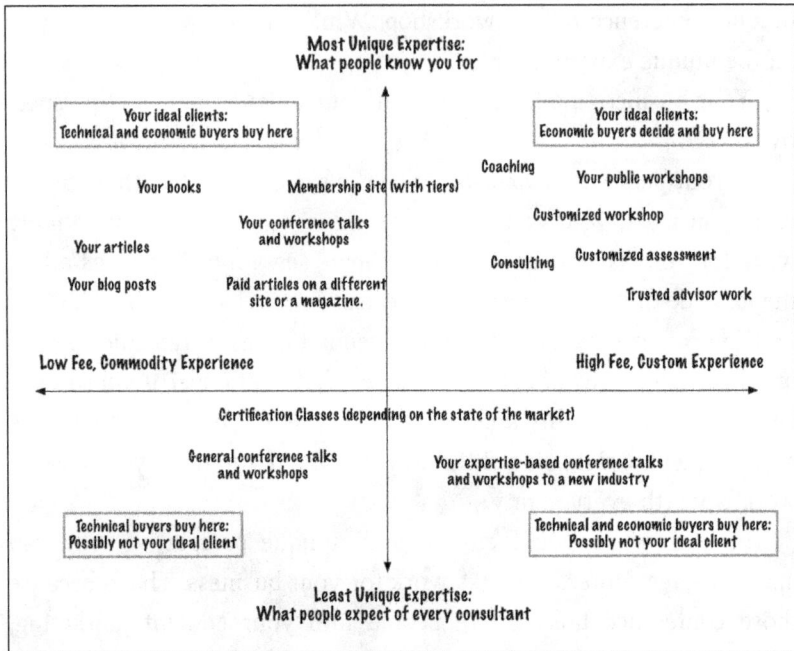

Figure 10.2: Possible Business Model

want and the state of the industry, those activities might help you discover technical buyers.

If you're a great speaker or writer, conference organizers and content managers will ask you to speak and write for them. Decide how much time *you* want to spend on low-fee experiences versus writing and speaking more for yourself.

Moving to the upper left quadrant, your ideal clients might discover you through more low-fee experiences:

- Newsletters, articles, blog posts on your site.
- Articles on other sites.
- Your books
- Lowest tier membership site.

While you exhibit your expertise and perspectives in your books, talks, and public conference workshops, you can't charge much for those activities. I recommend you use these upper left quadrant activities as a significant portion of how you create and share your expertise in public. That's where you can invite the audience into your upper right quadrant work.

The more people see you speak or read your writing, the more likely they are to move to the upper right quadrant, where they ask you to propose custom work for them.

If you decide to explore a new industry, you might find yourself in the lower right quadrant. You might not find the right mix of experiences to move to a new ideal client right away.

Here's what matters: the more income streams you have, especially those that span the upper left to the upper right quadrants, the more resilient your practice will be.

One of my highly technical colleagues limited his consulting practice to teaching highly technical workshops to technical teams. Through his week-long workshops, these teams learned agile practices to improve both their team experiences and products. His business model was: buy me a plane ticket and get me a hotel, and I'll fly anywhere in the world to work with your team.

Up until the pandemic, he was busy as often as he liked. He made plenty of money. Then, the pandemic hit. His only offerings were low-fee workshops or talks at conferences and high-fee workshops to teams. That was it.

As he said, "Before the pandemic, I made plenty of money. Now? I have no idea how to pay my mortgage."

It took him several months to recreate his workshops to work in a remote setting. And he had to decide which teams to work with and when, because he no longer worked with teams in their offices. He had to manage the time zone differences.

He succeeded, and now he offers several more options in the upper right quadrant, so he doesn't have to fly everywhere.

I suggested possible income streams earlier in this chapter. Consider which income streams you can create for your ideal clients:

Certification Classes Tend to Wax and Wane

Over the course of my career, I've seen many certifications come and go. When the certifications are new, the market is large. People (through their organizations) pay large sums of money to acquire that certification. (I'm not talking about licensing, this is a certification.)

However, most certifications become commodities over time. Unless you add your perspective or more value to each certification class, consider more income streams, possibly based on that certification, but not the certification offering itself.

- If you coach, can you offer individual, team, and management coaching? Remote and in-person?
- If you offer workshops, can you offer self-study remote workshops, interactive remote workshops, in-person workshops?
- If you speak as part of your business, can you create low-cost webinars, conference talks, custom speaking engagements for your clients, and keynotes for associations or larger conferences?
- Can you create various levels of membership products? (A membership product is an entry in your private or semi-private community. You might offer one level for free and several other paid levels.)
- If you write books, can you create custom books for your clients?

How can you slice and dice your expertise to offer products and services at all price points?

The more income streams you have, the more resilience you have in your business model. If possible, also consider passive income streams. Those passive streams help when consultants don't have enough clients.

10.3 **Create Passive Income Streams**

In *The Secrets of Consulting: A Guide to Giving and Getting Advice Successfully* WCO14, Weinberg says that consultants exist in one of two states: Idle or Busy. Idle is not enough business. Busy is too much business.

Regardless of the number of years of consulting you have, you too will find you are Idle or Busy—unless you diversify your income streams. In that case, you will likely have enough of one stream when another appears to vanish.

The market decides what commodity work is. And even terrific work can become commodity overnight. One day, you'll have plenty of work, and the next day, no one wants what you offer.

That's when passive income streams help with making money and cash flow.

Consider information products, such as books and self-study courses, as passive income streams.

What If You Have Too Much or Too Little Work?

If you have too much work, raise your fees. The clients who want to work with you will still choose you.

Sometimes, if you have too little work, raise your fees. If your potential clients think you're charging too little, they might not choose you for that work.

Low fees are no guarantee of more work. They certainly don't help you make more money. Review your value and the value you offer to your clients.

Anything you can make once and sell without your involvement and without changing is a candidate for a passive income stream.

10.4 Offer Consulting Based on Your Desired Consulting Role

Back in Chapter 1, Define Your Unique Value (p. 3), I said that consultants add different value based on the role they choose and I referenced McLendon's work.

You can choose a role and offer consulting based on that, especially if you choose a role that supports the client's growth, not results.

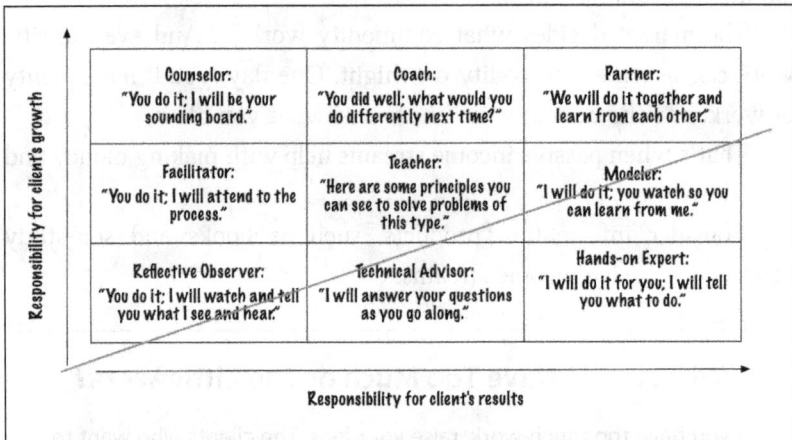

Figure 10.3: Consulting Roles Based on Client's Growth

I added a diagonal line to the original matrix, from the lower left to the upper right. The work under that diagonal line *tends* to be more commodity work. For example, when I took interim management roles, I was a hands-on expert who modeled effective management. I was happy to take that work because I could manage my schedule with small children.

During those engagements, I also hired my replacement. As that part of my consulting work, I used a combination of roles:

- I taught people how to hire, specifically managers.
- I facilitated their hiring process.
- I coached them in their hiring and interviewing process.
- I was a counselor helping them learn through discussion.

Several of my clients were thrilled to use me as an interim manager. That's because no other consultant offered to help hire their replacement. That was my unique value in those engagements.

The more you work as a Hands-on Expert, as a Modeler, or as a Technical Advisor, you place yourself in the lower right quadrant of the business model. Yes, this is honorable work and if you want to perform that work, terrific. However, clients tend to perceive that work as commodity work. Clients prefer to hire on an hourly basis for that work.

You might choose to take on Hands-on Expert work as you speak and write, establishing your expertise through content marketing. (That's what I did as an interim manager.) Then, the more you create your IP, the more you realize you can create offerings from that IP.

There's a big difference between Technical Advisor work and Trusted Advisor work.

As a technical advisor, the consultant answers client questions, often as the consultant watches the client. As a trusted advisor, consultants tend to ask the questions to aid the client in thinking through various situations. Trusted Advisors tend to work in the Counselor and Coach roles.

The more you work in the upper diagonal, the more unique your value is. That means you can charge more for that work.

As you define your products and services, consider the various ways you can showcase your unique expertise. You might want some commodity work as a floor for your business cash flow.

I can't tell you how many products and services you will require to create and sustain your successful consulting business. I do know that just one or two income streams is probably not enough. Seven or eight income streams might require more content marketing and might be too much.

However, consider how you can build resilience into how you make money.

That leads to the question of when to stop some work and still have a resilient business.

10.5 Stop Some Work and Continue to Make Money

Depending on how long you continue to consult, you might ask this question:

If I could no longer perform some part of my business, what would happen to my business?

Health insurance is part of the answer, but you have more options to continue to work, if you choose.

I like to think about this question in these ways:

- When the market no longer exists for me to do that work.
- When the work no longer interests or energizes me.
- When I can no longer physically do the work.

Here's how I've worked in these three areas for my consulting business.

10.5.1 *When the Market Vanishes*

I started writing this book during the COVID-19 pandemic. No one traveled for months, and certainly not for conferences. At that time, the conference market vanished.

Now, a couple of years later, some conferences have returned. However, attendance is down at many of the in-person conferences.

I know plenty of consultants who used conferences to attract clients. Once they attracted clients, they could book in-person workshops with those clients. Right *now*, that marketing approach doesn't work.

Markets do vanish overnight. I have lived through the dot-com bust, September 11, the recession of 2008, and now, the coronavirus.

In each case, I had substantial business booked with clients. Then, the market changed virtually overnight.

What happens if your market vanishes overnight?

- You might optimize "down" for quick cash. What can you do to make money, *now*? (Sometimes, that's commodity work, work that does not rely on your unique skills.)
- Instead of working with your current economic buyers, can you optimize "up" for the managers of those people?
- You might start to build your expertise for alternative industries or other ideal clients.

Other markets have vanished during my consulting career. For example, when I started consulting, many other consultants focused their business on various audit offerings. I'm sure some consultants still offer those services, but that business seems much smaller now.

For a while, "everyone" used waterfall approaches on their projects. I offered a unique perspective on how to organize projects differently. I made an excellent living rescuing projects from their waterfall disasters.

And, at this time, while "everyone" appears to use an agile framework, I make a nice living helping people think through and adapt their agile approach.

Every market trend vanishes at some point. And that means that when "everyone" goes one way, I tend to go the other. I build business resilience that way.

10.5.2 *When the Work no Longer Interests or Energizes You*

Sometimes, you develop expertise, and then, the work no longer interests you. You don't gain energy from doing the work. Worse, you're bored and might do the absolute minimum work.

If you realize the work no longer interests you, stop doing it. Remove that offering from your list.

As you review your financial results on a monthly and quarterly basis, look to see which offerings make you money. Are you still trying to use content marketing on work that no longer interests you or doesn't make you much money? That's work you can consider dropping. Alan Weiss in *Million Dollar Consulting: The Professional's Guide to Growing a Practice* WEI16 says to drop 15% of your work each year. While I don't measure the actual percentage, I do drop some work every year.

Instead of trying to maintain *that* work, use your content marketing to help you consider more and different offerings.

Does that mean you drop some of your clients? Maybe.

If you're doing work that no longer energizes you because a particular client wants that work, you're taking care of a client. Instead of taking care of your clients, take care of yourself.

Early in my consulting career, I focused on the quality and testing parts of projects and the organization. I soon realized I wanted to move farther upstream of that work. I also wanted to move further up the management hierarchy to be more influential. I started to speak about various kinds of management issues.

I value my experience in testing and quality. However, I dropped that work as I built my project, program, and portfolio expertise. My clients and I derive more value and satisfaction from my current work.

I changed the topics I wrote and spoke about so potential clients could see my expertise. My clients had to see evidence I understood what I offered as products and services. That's why I advocate you Keep Learning (p. 209).

You might get tired of some of your business. Watch for the commoditization of what you currently offer. Here's how I look at commodity work:

1. How many other people can offer this product or service as well—or better—than I? If there are several people I know, maybe it's time for me to drop this work and refer clients who want that work to those other people.

2. Can my clients see the difference in what I provide vs. what the other consultants provide? If not, can I create unique intellectual property? Or am I kidding myself, and the work is the same?

3. Do I need to rely on credentials or someone else to market me for this work? If so, I'm not creating my business model. They defined their business model, and I'm supporting them.

You might still want some of what I call commodity work, primarily if you teach certification classes or are new to consulting. Decide how much of that work composes all your products and services.

And, your clients can tell if the work you do no longer interests or energizes you. They will see that you don't want to be there. Choose a different set of work to serve them to the best of your ability.

Sometimes, you love the work, but you can't perform that work any longer.

10.5.3 *When I Can No Longer Do the Work*

I suffered an inner ear hemorrhage resulting in permanent vertigo in 2009. I continued to travel the world and consult for five years. In 2014, I realized I no longer had the energy for some of the work I had previously done. That's when I changed my mix of products and services.

I still travel the world—and I'm picky about when and where I travel. I don't automatically say yes to most requests as I might have in the past.

I have created other experiences—most of which I deliver online. When I don't have to travel, I can say yes to more options and retain my energy.

Although I was—and still am—a healthy consultant, sometimes, Things Happen. (This is one reason you must have excellent insurance: health insurance and short-term and long-term disability insurance. Do not scrimp on insurance.)

If you create a resilient consulting business, you can continue working and managing your life when those Things Happen. Also see Adapt and Evolve Your Successful Practice (p. 245).

10.6 Assess Your Business Model Over Time

In my experience, some event occurs every decade to change the market—which means you will change your business model.

I prefer to change my business model on my terms. Here are questions I ask myself about the work I consider:

- How will this work help me retain current clients?
- Can I use my expertise to acquire new and better clients?
- How can I create better experiences for my clients?
- Is there a way to offer work that helps me obtain revenue sooner?
- When do I choose to drop which work? Can I decide to create better and more fulfilling work for my clients and me?

Based on my unique expertise, I review and reassess the problems I solve for my clients—and how I deliver those solutions.

Those questions help me rethink my business model to change it, at minimum, yearly.

10.7 Now Do This to Examine How You Will Make Money

Consider how you want to make money.

In your consulting notebook:

1. Write down all your product and service offerings as part of your business model. Place them in the various axes of the business model image. See which products and services serve technical and economic buyers.
2. Check your definition of ideal client against your products and services.

3. How many income streams do you have now? Do you have the right number so you can make enough money?

Now that you have a draft business model and your products and services, prepare yourself for success by creating systems to manage your money.

CHAPTER 11

Manage Your Money

Before we start, I'm not a financial advisor. This chapter is not financial advice. You should always check with your accountant and possibly with your lawyer. In addition, check your local, state, and country laws to verify everything I suggest here.

As an employee, your employers paid you regularly and managed many of your tax payments. In the United States, they probably paid for your healthcare and training. In return, they paid you a salary. You learned to live within your budget, saving for the future.

Successful independent consultants not only need to pay themselves and manage their taxes and healthcare. In addition, they need to manage their expenses and plan their savings.

And if you're a new consultant, you might not know how to predict anything about money. Let's start there and address how to start your business with a bit of ease.

11.1 Start Your Business with Ease

Small businesses fail all the time. I'm sure you've seen many consultants who had to get a "real" job after a year or two of consulting. They might have started their business in a recession, during significant disruptive change, or not realized how much marketing they needed.

However, you can make it easier to start and stay a consultant:

1. Start with a financial cushion. Some consultants save a year's worth of their employee income before starting their consulting

business. Keep this money in liquid (easily accessible) funds if you do this.

2. Keep your fixed expenses low.
3. Start your content marketing as soon as you consider consulting—even before you "commit" to being a consultant.

These three actions will help you weather that first few months to a year. You won't have to take challenging clients or payment terms that might make you feel nervous.

Sometimes, you feel compelled to start your business even if you don't have a large cushion.

When I started my business, I had four weeks of my previous salary. That meant I worked hard to find speaking engagements and to start writing (content marketing). I also called everyone I knew to tell them I'd started my practice (active marketing).

I landed my first engagement within 60 days.

I *benefited* from the pressure of not quite enough money in the bank. I learned how to market and find clients. Because I wanted to contribute to our household finances, the pressure helped me learn how to create and propose reasonable fees. That kind of pressure might not help you.

I didn't use my small financial cushion except to maintain my haircuts, so I looked professional. However, I didn't buy any more equipment or clothing until I started to make more money.

When you start with a bit of financial ease, you might find it easier to maintain your financial health.

11.2 Maintain Your Financial Health

The first rule of business, assuming you want to stay in business, is this:

Manage Your Cash Flow.

Let's unpack that because I mean it in all these ways:

- Manage *expenses*, so you have enough money to choose: clients, which products and services you offer, when to work for a fee or free, when and where to take a vacation, and more.
- Gain *cash* through your mix of products and services—all your income streams.
- Make *cash flow* with your terms, so your clients pay you in a reasonable amount of time. Then you won't feel pressure when it's time to make your mortgage payment.

Employees can predict what money they will receive and when. Paying bills and budgeting for the future is relatively easy.

Consultants have more degrees of freedom: they choose their income streams, each with its relative value and compensation. And when consultants build that trusting relationship with their clients, they can create terms that everyone can live with.

Employers decide which products and services to offer. Based on all the employees' work, the company generates enough revenue to pay all the fixed and variable expenses for the business. Fixed expenses include rent and salary. Variable expenses can include supplies and electricity.

When employers want to manage expenses, they often reduce the variable costs. One of my long-ago employers decided to stop offering free coffee.

Sometimes, employers stop salary growth by creating a salary freeze, hiring freeze, or layoffs.

However, as an employee, you had some predictability for your income. You knew when the company would pay you. As a consultant, you take the responsibility for your income.

In my experience, the first thing that kills consultants is not understanding cash flow.

11.3 Understand Your Cash Flow

Cash flow—especially if it's negative—can kill your business.

Cash flow is your revenue minus all your expenses. Each of us incurs weekly, monthly, quarterly, and yearly expenses.

Let's start with a month at a time. Few consultants have a dependable monthly income. Yet, we often have recurring monthly expenses. That means we need to plan to smooth our cash flow.

Cash flow for consultants includes all these parts:

- Your fixed expenses: what it costs you to live and maintain your business. (Check with an accountant or lawyer to see how many of your living expenses you might charge to your business.)
- Your variable expenses: where else you choose to spend money.
- Your revenue and when you receive it.

In my experience, you have the most control over your fixed expenses. We'll start there.

11.3.1 *Assess Your Fixed Expenses*

Let's break fixed expenses into personal and business expenses. I'm assuming that your consulting company will not pay all your fixed *personal* expenses. You might be in a position to do so, and you *must* see a tax professional to decide how to manage your corporate structure and what's reasonable to deduct.

For example, I assume you have these personal expenses: rent or mortgage, individual health insurance, and phone. Your company will need to make enough money to cover these expenses, either with your salary or a distribution.

Your business also has expenses: any internet expenses so you can build and maintain your website, a phone for your business, and business-based insurance. I include my computer and printer in this category. See Start Your Business (p. 227) for more information about fixed business expenses.

Those are essential *fixed* expenses. (I'm not going to address depreciation here. Discuss depreciation with your accountant.)

I *regularly* assess my fixed expenses. The higher your fixed expenses, the more money you need to make in your business. For example, many software products have moved to a subscription model. You pay a monthly or yearly subscription to continue to use those products.

The more fixed expenses you have, the more money you need to earn.

In addition, you have expenses that would make your life easier. Those are variable expenses.

11.3.2 *Assess Your Variable Expenses*

Think back to the past month. Where did you have variable expenses? You might have bought some supplies. You buy them infrequently, so they're variable expenses. Maybe you registered for a three-month trial of new software. Until you decide you want to integrate that software into your toolset, that might be a variable expense. Maybe you took a workshop or bought a book.

These are all variable expenses. You don't incur them every single month. You choose to spend money when you have enough "extra" money to spend.

In *Cash Flow for Creators: How To Transform your Art Into a Career* LUC20, Michael Lucas breaks these expenses into these categories:

- Essential (your fixed expenses)
- Nice-to-have (your variable expenses)
- Total of both

I liked his ideas, so I created an example of how you might think of these expenses. See See Figure 11.1 Fictional Monthly Expenses on p. 178.

You *need* the cash flow in the Essential category. You *want* enough business to support the total of essential and nice-to-have expenses.

Successful consultants manage both fixed and variable expenses. Lucas encourages us to make a game out of our expenses. The point is to win the (Finance) Game by filling the Bucket (revenue) faster than your various costs empty the Bucket.

Cash flow: Expenses by Month				
Expense Category	Business expenses	Personal Expenses	Tax Estimates	Totals
Essential	Web site, internet, Business phone, Printer supplies, ... Example: $500	Base pay to cover rent, food, health insurance Example: $2000	Your base taxes Example: $500	Example: $3000
Nice-to-Have	Full business expenses: Logo designer, web site helper, marketing helper Example: $500	Full pay, vacation away from home, more tv channels Example: $1000	$1000	Example: $2500
Example totals	$1000	$3000	$500-1000 with cushion	$3000-5500 with cushion

Figure 11.1: Fictional Monthly Expenses

I pay a few hundred dollars a year for my website, various cloud storage, backup, and other software services in the cloud. If you're starting your business, you might choose to use the free versions of these services. However, once you make enough revenue, revisit those decisions. Sometimes, the paid versions offer more features, security, and resilience.

Most of the time, I get substantial value from the lowest tier of the service. That allows me much more cloud storage, better video meetings, and constant backup. I don't have to worry about insufficient storage, meetings that disconnect, or inadequate backup. I have peace of mind, knowing my tools serve my business.

Invest enough in your business that you have peace of mind.

If you worry about spending money on subscriptions and services, create a spreadsheet and add all your subscription costs. Could you offer a low-fee product or service that would offset these expenses?

You might find that you have money "leaks." You don't mean to spend the money, but you do. I tend to discover leaks as part of my variable expenses.

Learn Your Money Leaks

I'm a sucker for office supplies. I have enough pens and stickies to supply several consultants for several years. That's a money leak in my business. You might have a different leak, such as fancy coffee.

Track those expenses on a daily, weekly, and monthly basis. Daily and weekly small expenses add up over the course of a year.

But sometimes, the biggest offenders are the yearly subscriptions. For example, most of us use online cloud storage and several online applications. Those providers charge a yearly fee, often based on tiers. Assess your current use of that provider and whether you need the same tier or not.

Assess all your subscriptions and small expenses at least once a year. Before you start leaking money.

Here's how I look for my money leaks:

- Every time I pay cash for an expense, I review what remains in my wallet. Or, I take the receipt and assign that cost to the correct cost category in my money application.
- I check my credit cards and assign every charge to a specific cost category.
- Every month, I review my various categories. Am I overspending? Underspending? What might I need to change?

Assess your monthly expenses, especially if you want to manage your costs. What could you eliminate? Every consultant I've met has had to decide what's essential and what's nice to have. Watch for your money leaks.

Once you understand your expenses, look for deductible expenses.

11.3.3 *Understand Deductible Expenses*

This section is not financial advice. You should see your financial advisor, a tax advisor, or an accountant for their advice. This section is my experience only.

You can take advantage of tax deductions to manage some of your business expenses. Here's a partial list of what I can deduct from my gross income to reduce taxes:

- All software subscriptions and purchases for software I use in my business.
- My internet connection, website, and all expenses associated with my site.
- All my books because I write both non-fiction and fiction in short and long forms.
- Office supplies.

In the US, right now, you can only deduct business expenses if you file your taxes as a business. (I don't know about other countries.)

While I don't depend on deductible expenses to manage my cash flow, I do gain some value from these deductions.

Remember, the more costs you have, the more money you *have* to make. And that means you might feel as if you must take specific work, just to pay expenses.

If you manage all your expenses, you might find more flexibility in selecting clients and work. Regardless of this, always speak with your accountant about what you can deduct in your tax jurisdiction.

While deductions help manage taxes, I much prefer to increase my income. That's why I suggest you track the revenue you associate with each income stream, not units.

11.4 Track Revenue, Not Units

Some consultants count their client trips, the number of keynotes, or the number of workshops they sell.

These measures are vanity metrics because they don't offer any predictability for monthly or yearly revenue.

Consider these two numbers:

- Your overall revenue, broken down by income stream.
- Your overall expenses.

When consultants track revenue by income stream, they can decide how well each stream contributes to their overall revenue. Then, they can review their satisfaction with those streams.

Armed with data about each income stream, you can decide to stop, continue, or change your streams. If you decide to stop that stream, you might not need to *do* anything, except create more content for a different stream.

If you plan to continue that stream, you might add more content marketing to promote that stream.

And if you decide to change a stream, you might decide to learn more, add more content marketing, or even change what you offer now.

Sometimes, I experiment with new income streams when I speak to meetups or professional groups. The audience's reaction to the content helps me decide if I want to add this IP to my streams.

Beware of vanity metrics. Track the revenue from each of your streams.

Now, you'll see how well you're managing your revenue and expenses when you write your checks yourself.

11.5 Write the Checks Yourself

You gain a deep visceral understanding of your cash flow when *you* deposit the client's check and when *you* pay your expenses. When you see money flow in and out of your business, you see your financial reality.

Retain control of your checkbook, and you retain control of your business.

If you're unsure how to use the various software applications to keep your books, you might want a bookkeeper, but that person becomes an additional expense when you need to keep your fixed expenses low. Instead, buy a manual or a book about small business bookkeeping.

Sometimes, you can use your life partner as your bookkeeper. However, you need total trust with your partner. (Full disclosure: my husband is now my bookkeeper. I was my bookkeeper for the first 20 years of my business.)

Except for you, no one understands the difference between your essential and non-essential expenses. Clarify your necessary and non-essential expenses with your life partner. Have those conversations before you give your checkbook to anyone else.

Otherwise, manage your checking account yourself.

When you allow someone else to manage your checkbook, you invite that person into your business. Be wary of that expense until you are well-established and have some predictability in your consulting business.

I recommend against a bookkeeper when you start your business.

11.6 Decide How You Will Pay Yourself

At some point, you pay yourself a salary. You can also pay yourself a distribution. Talk to your accountant about how your state and country tax these two kinds of payments.

Because I'm based in the US, I use a payroll service. That way, I always know I'm paying and filing the correct forms on time. Different countries have different rules, so be aware of your rules.

Make sure you account for paying yourself as you manage your money.

11.7 Don't Let Your Clients Manage Your Money

In Create Successful Proposals (p. 89), I suggested you always ask for a 50% deposit with the remainder net 30, or a discount for payment in full in advance of the work. If you do not set those terms—or better—you might end up allowing your clients to manage your money.

Clients are people. Often, these people work in large organizations with "policies." Those policies create boundaries about how much you can charge per day, the kinds of expenses they will reimburse you for, and when they will pay you after receiving your invoice.

The finance people believe these policies. Often, the HR people do, too. However, the economic buyer *can* manage these policies.

Whatever you do, don't let your clients bully you into accepting terms longer than 30 days. You will finish your work long before the terms they want you to accept. What are you going to do, rescind your report? Or your advice?

You can always decline the offer to work with these people. Or, you can add a sufficiently large "tax" to your original fee to live with the net 60 or 90 days these companies think they can use.

Make sure you are happy if you get the work and happy if you don't. But don't let your clients manage your cash flow.

11.8 Evaluate Requests for Free Work

If you speak and write enough, people will ask you for copies of your books, courses, or anything else for free. They want your work to affiliate themselves and their work with you.

Make sure you evaluate these requests. I use a mix of context-free and contextual questions to evaluate these requests:

- What value does each of us gain if I fulfill this request?
- What value does each of us lose if I fulfill this request?
- What does success look like for each of us if I fulfill this request?
- What problems does this create for either of us if I fulfill this request?

- Why do you want me to do this?

These are an adaptation of context-free questions. In reality, they reveal a lot about the other person's context.

What if people want you to speak for "free"? If you need to travel, prepare something special for them, or otherwise take time out of your day, ask the questions above to clarify why you should or should not speak for their group.

I often speak locally or remotely for free—assuming the organizers don't charge for attendance. If I'm at a conference in another city, I offer to talk at a local meetup or professional group, because I'm already there.

Free work often costs you working time, so evaluate it carefully. Successful independent consultants choose what to do and when. That includes when to hire helpers for your business.

11.9 When Should You Hire People?

Some consultants hire virtual assistants for continual support. Others hire people for specific tasks. These are both examples of contractors, work for hire.

If you're thinking of hiring someone, either as an employee or a contractor, ask yourself:

How many days of consulting do I need to work to pay this person?

If you realize you need help in your business, think carefully:

- Can you automate this task, so you don't need someone else?
- Can you create a system to manage this kind of work, as I do with my schedule?
- How can you document this work, so the person you hire can complete the work to your satisfaction?

As soon as you hire someone, you've added to your fixed expenses. Be careful about adding to those expenses. That question, "How much do I need to work to afford this person?" has saved me plenty of money over the years.

11.10 Now Try This to Manage Your Money

Remember, I'm not offering financial advice. Always check with your financial advisor, accountant, or tax advisor for your local rules.

Consider these ideas to manage your money.

1. Create a spreadsheet to assess your personal and business fixed expenses, weekly, monthly, and yearly. What is the minimum monthly amount you need to exist? How much money would you like to make your life easier?
2. Assess all your variable expenses, weekly, monthly, yearly. Do you have leaks anywhere?
3. Think back to the last three times someone asked you to work for "free" or otherwise donate your time or work. What did you receive in return?

Don't allow your money to manage your choices. Manage your money so you can choose how you work.

Part of that choice is how you will stay healthy, not only financially, but physically and emotionally.

CHAPTER 12

Manage Your Health

You can't serve your clients if you don't maintain your financial, physical, and emotional health.

We discussed your financial health in the previous chapter. Now, it's time for your physical and emotional health and how to create systems to build and maintain your health.

Have you ever worked with an excellent team? I have. Aside from knowing what we needed to do, we supported each other. We collaborated on solving all kinds of problems and offered feedback and coaching.

We had collegial relationships, where we supported each other.

Even if you've only experienced one or two of those teams, you felt your teammates' support.

As independent consultants, we have to make our own kinds of support. I'll talk about a professional support system later in this chapter, but for now, let's discuss how you might need support from your family.

12.1 Enlist Your Family for Support

I assume you have already discussed the risks of becoming a consultant with your family and that they are ready to support you. (If you haven't yet discussed those risks, make sure you do. Or see a professional counselor so you can discuss those risks.)

I also assume you have a relatively healthy relationship with your family, where you all support each other's self-esteem. If your family decimates your self-esteem, consider seeing a counselor or somehow creating a better environment for yourself.

Our families can support us in these ways when we have conversations about:

- Family and business finances, especially the fixed and variable expenses for the business and the family.
- Everyone's professional and school responsibilities, especially for work time and travel.
- Life responsibilities, especially for other people such as children, parents, and pets.

When I say "discuss" that includes the consequences on your business.

When I first started to work from home, my mother said, "Oh, you can start a load of laundry whenever you have to."

I said, "No, laundry is for Sundays. Monday through Friday is for work." (Back when my children were small, my husband and I created routines. We still use those routines because they work for us. I am sure you are more flexible than we are.)

When my children still lived at home, my husband and I managed our travels. One of us was always home—we didn't need childcare support.

My husband and I negotiated who would cook which days and drive the various carpools.

When it was time for our children to go to university, we discussed how much we had saved and what we could afford—and we included the children in these discussions. Because we had saved for retirement and university through the years, we could make reasonable decisions for us.

My family supported my consulting business, which allowed me to thrive as a consultant. I could serve both my clients and family.

You might need different discussions. Maybe you have pets or older family members who need your support.

Or, maybe your family isn't very supportive of your desire to be a consultant. In that case, make sure you discuss expenses—regularly.

12.1.1 Discuss Expenses

If you are the primary money provider for the family, you'll need your family's support to reduce your fixed expenses.

Ask Your Family to Reduce Expenses

Years ago, Al, a consulting colleague, hustled to get clients. He didn't think he had time for content or active marketing, so he subcontracted for a large consulting company. If they didn't "fill" his weeks, he also used recruiters for what he called "side gigs."

Even though he worked all the time, he thought he made "almost" enough money. I asked, and he told me—a substantial six-figure income.

In a consulting conversation, I suggested he needed better clients who would pay him more money for less time, especially travel time. He could decline some work and spend time content marketing.

"I can't," he said. "My wife won't give up our way of life."

His fixed expenses were killing him—and his consulting business. And because he didn't ask his wife for her support, Al decided to become an executive at a large organization. That management work wasn't as fulfilling as he wanted. But, he didn't have to travel all the time, and he could support his wife the way they *both* desired.

Al didn't ask her for support. I'm not sure if he didn't think he could or he didn't want to. And, his wife didn't offer support or to change.

If you ever avoid difficult discussions about expenses, you'll never know how your family *will* support you. Have those difficult conversations.

Sometimes, it's easier to discuss client problems than discuss challenges with our family members. I suspect that we don't realize that asking for help requires strength.

12.1.2 *Learn to Ask for Help*

If you feel pressure as Al did, you can learn to ask for help.

Many societies reward independence, where we can say, "I did it all by myself." Except, very few consultants can say that.

We need our families to support us when our business isn't going well: we can't find enough clients; we're not sure we can deliver the proposed work; or we worry about money. When business isn't going well, we might feel a lack of self-esteem.

When I feel a lack of self-esteem is precisely when I need help. Here's why you should ask for help from your family:

- You offer them a gift. Most families want to help and support you. Even your children might want to support you. When you ask for their support, you offer them a gift.
- You admit you don't know everything, and that makes it easier for you to support your clients better.
- You create space for new possibilities so that you can learn. Your family might have terrific marketing ideas or places to network.

The more you enlist your family for support, the more options you can create for your business.

Part of those options includes time with and away from your family.

12.1.3 *Manage Your Time Away from the Family*

We have many opportunities to work long and hard. So one of the big questions for consultants is when and how much you will work:

- Which days will you work and when?
- Are the weekends off-limits for work?
- How about the weeknights? Do you participate in professional meetups during the week?

If we don't manage our work times and durations, we might burn out or otherwise affect our mental health.

I like a routine for my days: my workout times, my breakfast, lunch, and dinner times, and especially my work start and end times. And, I flex those times when I work with international clients.

I work a five-day week, with several breaks each day to walk and exercise. My day looks a lot like any employee's day, except that my commute is just fourteen steps down the hall. During the workday, I work.

If you have responsibilities for young children or aging parents, you might have to change your work hours. These items changed my work hours when my children were young:

- Carpools for the childrens' activities.
- Their holidays and vacation weeks.

After much discussion, my husband and I decided that while the children were young, I would take time off my work to take care of them. We created a family calendar and discussed who would travel and when.

We often used the "first on the calendar gets that travel time" algorithm. And, we supported each other and discussed what we could and could not change.

When we chose our family vacation time, I also blocked those days off on my calendar. I do not work on vacation.

Everyone needs a vacation. Schedule your vacation time every year.

I never wanted to be in the position of trading vacation or family time for client work.

However, part of my *work* time is professional volunteering or meetup attendance.

12.1.4 *Manage Professional Volunteering*

How much time will you spend volunteering or at professional meetups? Do you want to negotiate that time with your family?

I discovered that volunteering for local professional groups helped me network with people and honed my facilitation skills.

(You haven't lived until you've facilitated a volunteer group whose members disagree on the reason why the group exists. Well, maybe you have.)

Most of the time, these meetings included supper and lasted until about 9:00 p.m. Sometimes, the meetings lasted longer.

You'll have to decide if these volunteer opportunities fit for you. I estimate I gained several hundred thousand dollars of consulting business because I had a public face. The volunteer activities helped me network with local people to obtain local work.

12.1.5 *Manage the Rest of Your Family*

Not everyone understands how much energy and time you need to start and maintain a thriving business. You might have extended family with (loud!) opinions about when you work, what you do, and how much time you spend with the people in your house.

I didn't choose to discuss my money decisions or consulting practice with my extended family. You might choose differently.

I did ask for support, and I received it. My father-in-law bought me my first book about consulting—Howard Shenson's *Guide to Consulting Success.*

If you've never started a business before, discuss all of these issues with your family. Make sure you gain their support for your business time. And, make sure you support the family as you choose your family time.

In addition, we can learn how to ask for help from other people. That might serve you very well in a client engagement.

One big way to create a thriving business is to learn with other consultants.

12.2 **Learn with Colleagues**

The motivational speaker, Jim Rohn, said that we are the average of the five people we spend the most time with. If that's even close to true, then successful independent consultants should manage who they spend time with and how.

Consider forming learning groups with colleagues. Ask for and offer feedback on writing and workshops. Maybe even co-create articles and workshops. Then, practice learning how to develop and teach together. Reflect on each of these experiences, to make sure you all benefit from the collaboration.

I was fortunate and spent more than a decade consciously learning with Jerry Weinberg, Esther Derby, and Don Gray, along with several other wonderful people. We created a conference. As a learning cohort, we learned to:

- Write conference proposals and how to offer feedback to each other.
- Market the conference and ourselves.
- Create interactive workshops that supported the participants' learning.

While we made a little money from the conference, that wasn't the point. The conference itself was a form of content marketing. The participants could see us and use our expertise. That marketing brought us many more clients.

I enjoyed that learning cohort experience so much that I continue to practice learning with others, writing books and offering public workshops.

12.3 Build Your Learning Support System

I also have a support system from my fellow consultants. I use my colleagues for feedback and coaching—and they often ask me for the same. We also purposefully learn together, either by offering events or planning for learning.

You might think I'm "lucky." I have worked to be lucky. I always sought out other consultants for collaboration and especially for learning. I'd experienced cohort-based learning at work before, and I wanted that again with fellow consultants.

My current success is a product of my learning with other consultants.

Find ways to build your community of like-minded consultants so you can learn together and support each other. While your family can support you, they are not the right people to use as a learning support system.

Now that you've reflected on your emotional and learning health, consider how you will keep your body healthy.

12.4 Plan Your Physical Health

Consultants tend to travel a lot. And, part of traveling is early and late flights, long hours working, insufficient exercise, and eating the wrong food. I've been in too many airports with delayed flights where my only option was fast food.

While I enjoy the taste of fast food, I don't enjoy the long-term effects of eating too much fast food.

Sometimes, consultants sit a lot. Even with a great ergonomic setup, you might not realize when your back or wrists get sore—until it's too late.

That's why I plan my physical health, just as much as I plan my financial health.

I work to maintain my necessary hours of sleep, manage my work time, get enough exercise, and eat right.

I choose my hotels so I can stay healthy when I travel. Do you need a hotel with exercise equipment or a pool?

I also choose hotels with a reputation for sufficient wifi and comfortable beds. If you don't have adequate wifi, you'll stay up too late or have to wake too early to finish that last-minute work. (Even better, don't do last-minute work.)

Only you can know the right and wrong food for you. Find an eating plan that you can follow and that works for you. A low-fat eating plan was a disaster for me. I've followed a low-carb plan for many years and can maintain my weight, even with travel.

Learn what works for you and make reasonable choices for yourself.

Make Your Own Travel Arrangements

Many years ago, a client in San Francisco offered to make travel arrangements for my visit. I gave the client the parameters, and their travel people ignored all those parameters.

As a result, the six-hour direct flight turned into a three-stop fourteen-hour day. And because they used a third-rate hotel, I only had a room for one night with no wifi.

The next day, I took an hour to book a reasonable hotel and rebook my flight back home. Clients might think they're saving money. Instead, they make everything more difficult when they don't create a good travel experience for you.

You can't serve your clients long-term if you don't stay healthy. That goes for your emotional health, too.

12.5 Assess Your Emotional Health

Consultants face client rejection all the time. Potential clients don't call back, or they reject your ideas. Or, they say you're too expensive because they didn't realize their problems required your value.

I wrote a little about Imposter Syndrome, and the Dunning-Kruger effect in Define Your Unique Value (p. 3). In addition, you will need to assess and sustain your self-esteem. Consider the Satir self-esteem toolkit in Weinberg's *More Secrets of Consulting: The Consultant's Toolkit* WCM14.

I also recommend these books to help you find ways to think about your mental models:

- Carol Dweck's *Mindset: The New Psychology of Success* DWE07

- Barbara Fredrickson's *Positivity: Top-Notch Research Reveals the 3-to-1 Ratio That Will Change Your Life* FRE09
- Marty Seligman's *Learned Optimism: How to Change Your Mind and Your Life* SEL06

I'm not a mental health professional. If you have emotional health issues, make sure you learn your patterns and what you can do. And don't be afraid to ask for help from a professional.

I know I'm doing something exciting and new when I get a little nervous. I can take that nervousness and turn it into excitement.

I know I'm out of my league when I become anxious, and that's when I ask for help. In addition, I start the work early so I can succeed, regardless of my anxiety. When I finish work and progress every day, I can manage that anxiety. I am not you, so learn what works for you.

Learn your emotional patterns and how you can manage those patterns so you can thrive.

12.6 Tips to Manage Your Health

If you've only worked for companies, you might not realize how creating your own business can challenge your self-esteem. When I work with consultants, I often discover how they *feel* about money can help or hurt them emotionally.

These tips might help you decide what to discuss with the people who can offer your support.

- Decide what "enough" money is.
- Work for satisfaction, not money alone.

Let's start with "enough" money.

12.6.1 Tip: Decide What "Enough" Money Is for You

In the previous chapter, I suggested you could start your business with a financial cushion to make life easier for you. In addition, consider how much money you want to make.

I've created a business that more than replaces my original salary. And I've worked hard to achieve that outcome. While I *grossed* more than my original salary my first full year in business, I had overhead expenses that meant I didn't entirely replace my salary.

However, I have seen some people make significant revenue in their first year as consultants:

- They'd already written a book that made them famous. (Isn't that wonderful when that happens?) They created talks and workshops about the book.
- They'd been speaking and writing for years. They published articles, blogs, and books. They spoke at conferences regularly. They'd already started their content marketing work. When they became consultants, they found it easy to attract clients.
- They taught high-priced certification classes. They often taught two to three weeks a month.

I started consulting before I wrote my first book. And I wasn't lucky enough that one of my books made me famous. Maybe you can be that lucky.

I've seen the speak-and-write before consulting model work well for about a dozen people. I didn't realize I needed to write and speak before becoming a consultant, or I might have used that approach.

The rest of us need to learn how to use content marketing to attract clients. Once you do that, you'll make enough money. Maybe not in your first year of consulting, but you will.

However, you do need to decide what's enough for you.

Set a "Greed Line" for Revenue

Alistair Cockburn, a well-known agile consultant explained his "greed line:"

"My wife and I managed our expenses. We chose a reasonable revenue goal for me." When I hit that goal, we realized more money

> wouldn't make us happier or make our lives better. I made the rule, "Once I hit the greed line, ANYTHING has higher priority than the next gig."
>
> He hit his greed line each year in the fall. That's when he chose to decide what to do for the rest of the year.

The more you set your fixed expenses and the more you use project- or value-based fees, the faster you get to the greed line. The more time you have to create more IP that helps your clients find you.

And, if you're working all the time for a client, you're not learning or taking a vacation. Or relaxing.

You owe yourself a sustainable business. That means you charge clients what you're worth for agreed-upon outcomes. You understand what success means for you. And you work for your satisfaction, too.

12.6.2 *Tip: Work for Satisfaction*

If you think about the "greed line," you might realize you want to offer different products and services.

For example, maybe you wrote a terrific book. You've traveled the world, offering talks, consulting, workshops based on the book. You've made a lot of money.

And, at some point, you look at your work, and you say, "I wish I could do something else. I'm tired of this."

If you work for money *alone*, you might not be satisfied after a while. Everyone can tell when your work no longer satisfies, energizes, or excites you.

That's exactly the time to drop a portion of your business so you can create more IP around another aspect of your expertise. Review your business model and work for satisfaction, not just money.

12.7 **Now Try This to Manage Your Health**

We use our emotions, intellect, and physical capabilities in every client interaction. Learn how to keep yourself healthy.

In your consulting notebook, write this down:

1. What conversations do you need to have with your family about family time and money? When can you have those conversations?
2. Are you happy with your time with and away from your family now? If not, what alternatives can you create?
3. How will you build collegial relationships with other consultants so that you can learn together?
4. What do you need to do to create a system of physical health and sleep?
5. How do you recognize when you are emotionally off-kilter? Do you know how to find a better emotional place? If not, what do you need to learn?

Now that all aspects of your health have been looked after, decide how you will organize your calendar.

CHAPTER 13

Manage Your Calendar

You might worry—how can you get "everything" done?

As an employee, the company dictated a lot about your day. Someone else set deliverables and probably told you when to deliver that work. Your company expected you to work "core hours" and attend various meetings. In addition, too many managers overrode your calendar to schedule more meetings.

That all changes when you work for yourself.

You decide on your deliverables and when you will finish them. You'll choose when to work and which meetings to attend. No one will override your calendar meetings.

You have the freedom to work differently and the responsibility to do so. That freedom and responsibility might feel strange.

Consider how you will assess your capacity for all the work you choose:

- Which products and services you offer and how you fulfill them,
- When and how you market,
- And any other work activities that create or fulfill business.

You can succeed when you see your capacity and sustain a regular working pace.

I recommend you use the big picture planning you did back in Decide How You Will Make Money (p. 157) and Create Your Marketing Plan (p. 44).

I use my calendar to create daily and weekly deliverables to succeed. I recommend you do, too.

First, let's start with the idea that we manage our actions, not time.

13.1 Manage Your Actions

A lot of people talk about "time management."

I don't buy that. We each have the same amount of time in a day. When we choose our actions, we decide what to spend time on.

Consider reframing time management as "action management." I first learned that term from David Allen, author of *Getting Things Done: The art of stress-free productivity* ALL15.

When we decide what's essential and finish small chunks of work, we can finish more than we can imagine. We choose which actions to take and when. In addition, I plan my work for a given day to make sure I finish *something* every day. That's because none of us can do it "all."

Here's how I organize my actions:

- I write down everything I want to do, especially if I have a lot going on. I happen to use paper. You might like an electronic tool. Regardless of how you write down, do not rely on your memory to track your work. Allen says, "Your head is a lousy office." I write down my work as many small deliverables.
- I rank the work by what's most valuable to me. Sometimes, I have time-critical work, such as a proposal. That rises to the top.
- If all the work looks as if it's the same value, I ask myself if I can spend 15 minutes and finish something I can deliver to myself—or make enough progress that I can stop that work for now. That's how I progress through a significant deliverable, such as a book or a workshop.
- I sometimes schedule time in my calendar to do strategic work but lower in importance right now. I often have a book in progress. Book-writing is high strategic value but low

immediate tactical value work. That's because every book I write offers me new ways to change my business model—but only once I finish the book.

I use a daily rhythm of working from about 9 a.m. to about 6 p.m. My schedule looks a lot like anyone's "regular" job.

In addition, I use a lean approach called flow to make sure I don't have too much WIP (Work in Progress) or that I let work languish. And I regularly reflect on my work to see if I want to change something about my work or plans. I use that reflection to replan.

Working in flow might sound familiar to you if you're familiar with agile or lean approaches. I use personal kanban as in, *Personal Kanban: Mapping Work | Navigating Life* BEN11 to create daily and weekly plans.

You don't have to use personal kanban. Instead, you might create actions in your calendar.

As you plan, ask yourself this question: Can I create several deliverables for myself today and finish them? When I do, I can get into the flow of the work and finish faster. See *Flow: The Psychology of Optimal Experience* CSI08.

Because I don't plan much at any time, planning doesn't take me very long. And, because I like finishing chunks of work, I tend to work in 15- to 20-minute timeboxes.

A timebox is a specific limited time you have to accomplish a particular deliverable. I use timeboxes to manage my progress on "everything." I don't work on "everything" at one time. Instead, I choose one item to work on for now and get that work to some relative "done" state.

The more you practice creating small deliverables, the more you'll see how. You can use this knowledge to help your clients, too. Your clients probably have too-large chunks for their work.

However, every consultant has unplanned work. Consider how you want to manage that unexpected work.

13.2 **Manage Unplanned Work**

Your potential clients will call you to discuss possible work. You already planned your week, so that call is unplanned work.

Or, you learn about a new-to-you conference where you might meet more ideal clients. So you decide to propose a session—also unplanned work. These reasons are why I leave room in my daily and weekly calendar for unplanned work.

When I first started to consult, I counted my various chunks of work. I had data that said I could complete three chunks of work every day, fifteen chunks per week. I *planned* for only ten of those chunks, leaving five chunks per week unplanned.

Because I didn't over-plan my week, I felt comfortable about my ability to finish one chunk and then choose another piece of work.

I use a paper board—not an electronic tool. That physical limitation restricts the amount of work I can put on the board. The paper board limits my WIP (Work in Progress). The board helps me avoid planning for too much work in one day or week.

I also keep a monthly backlog of options I want to consider. I don't have to commit to those options early—I leave room for better choices as time goes on.

Because I don't have a lot on my weekly board, I feel as if I finish work fast. That finishing allows me to pull new work from the monthly backlog or the parking lot. (For more information about project portfolio management, see *Manage Your Project Portfolio: Increase Your Capacity and Finish More Projects, 2nd ed* ROT16.)

Every so often, I realize I'm not going to get to an action I thought I could do this week or this month. Or, I don't want to lose the work, but I don't have time for it now. I move that work to the parking lot, the list of options.

The parking lot allows me to look at the list and *choose* whether to tackle any of those projects. I don't lose the ideas and I can create options for future work.

Content marketing means I often have many more ideas than I can execute at one time. That creates my need to focus:

- My weekly kanban helps me focus on what I need to do *this* week.
- My monthly backlog is a guide for what I thought I would want to do when I planned.
- The parking lot is where I put ideas I might not want to lose, but I'm not going to do now.

Because I don't distract myself with future work, the monthly backlog and the parking lot help me remain focused on the day-to-day work.

You might choose to review your parking lot weekly or monthly, as you plan. When you review it, decide what you no longer want to consider.

13.3 Plan with Your Board and Calendar

I use my board to see what I need to do today and this week and I add those items to my calendar. Then, if I happen to finish something early, I can pull an item from my board. I right-size my work so I don't overschedule myself and have time for unexpected events, such as discovery calls. I also use my calendar to schedule time for high-priority actions.

Right-sizing the work allows me to work at a steady pace, not too much for one day and not too little. Some people estimate their work. I don't. Instead, I use hourly timeboxes and see what I accomplished in that time. That allows me to chunk the rest of my work and count the timeboxes I need to finish.

Here's an example. Imagine you plan to visit a client to deliver a three-day workshop in three weeks. You already wrote parts of that workshop in various forms: talks, blog posts, and articles. And you realize you need to add more content.

How long will it take to complete that workshop? I never quite know, but I use the guideline of planning for three hours of preparation for every workshop hour. I also know the deadline, so for my mental ease, I want to complete the workshop by the end of the second week. That way, I've built in a little slack.

I recommend you do something like this:

- Block 30-60 minutes of time in your calendar, starting the first day. As an example, 10 - 11 a.m.
- Assess where you are at the end of that time. Do you need more time on Monday to meet your deadline? If so, consider blocking hours at 2 and 4 p.m.
- Continue blocking enough hours every day so you can complete the workshop preparation.

You might wonder about those breaks and if they encourage you to multitask. They do, and, because consultants are also managers, successful consultants learn to break large projects into smaller deliverables, finish those deliverables, and move to the next bit of work.

In addition, those breaks allow you to learn from what you did earlier. Every time we create a product or piece of content, we learn. When we take a short break, we can more easily integrate that learning. And learn what we don't know yet.

What if you don't have the content already? You would need more time. But why would a client choose you if you don't already use those topics for content marketing?

I create recurring tasks, such as my newsletter, on my calendar. That way, I have a better chance of remaining consistent in writing and sending them.

13.4 Reflect Daily on Your Work

You might want to reflect daily to see that you accomplish what you need to accomplish. I ask two specific questions almost every day about waste and my board:

Did I waste time today because I didn't want to do something?

Sometimes, I waste time because I let something distract me. Sometimes, I waste time because I feel overwhelmed. I like to understand why I wasted time.

If I wasted time, I ask myself several questions:

- Is the work so extensive that I can't see how to start? If so, what's the first chunk that I can do in 15 minutes that will let me see what to do next?
- Am I the right person for that work? When I needed to revamp my website, I wasted weeks before realizing I needed professional help. Once I got that help, the work proceeded much faster.
- Do I need to do this work now? Maybe I would be better off if I put that work on the parking lot to do later.
- Should I remove that work altogether? Sometimes, we postpone work, and there's no point in considering it. Or, we're too early with an idea, and we don't see a market for it.

Between client work and content marketing, I have no end of work. I want to make sure I choose the most valuable work at all times.

I also ask this question:

Is my board working for me?

I've used personal kanban for years. And as my work has changed, I've changed my board. The more often I reflect on how I use my tools, the faster I can decide to experiment.

Since I'm human, I make mistakes with my planning. However, when I reflect daily, I can see where I progress and where I don't.

13.5 Reflect Weekly on Your Work

I also recommend you reflect weekly on your goals, what you completed and what's remaining for you to complete. For me, the daily reflection is tactical. I use the weekly reflection to address my strategy.

I like to ask myself these questions:

1. How long did I expect each piece of work to take? How long did the work actually take?
2. How much of what kinds of work did I finish last week? (Of my content marketing and any other work, what did I finish and not finish?)
3. How much work did I start and finish for my content marketing?
4. What did I not start that I thought I would start? Does that work belong on the parking lot? Should I delete that work or find someone to do that work for me?
5. Where do I want to go next week for what I want to do?

You might have other questions about your work. Reflect at least weekly and learn from your data. Your data will help you manage your following actions.

Should *You* Do All Your Work?

I'm not a fan of hiring people to help you in your business, especially when you start. And, as you proceed, you might realize you're not going to do this particular work. You need help to accomplish that work.

As you reflect on the work you didn't do, make sure you can complete that work. If you can't finish that work, decide if you should learn the work or hire someone to do it for you.

As you reflect each day and week, learn your patterns. What do you spend the most time on? Does that effort pay off for you? Would you be better off if you spent time elsewhere?

In my experience, successful independent consultants spend much of their time learning and marketing. The learning is about how you increase your value. The marketing is so your clients can find you.

13.6 Schedule Longer Reflections

I do a little retrospective for my plans every month, quarter, and year. Am I finishing the most valuable work for my business? Am I learning?

In December, to plan for the next year, I make sure to put this work on my board:

- What work will I drop to do more interesting and challenging work?
- Review my newsletter automation to make sure it's accurate.
- Can I generate twelve newsletter topics now? I don't have to write those newsletters. However, with this small amount of preparation, I never stare at a blank page.

You might need different reflection times. In my experience, daily and weekly reflections aren't enough. Decide what works best for you.

13.7 Schedule Time to Learn and Market

Regardless of how you organize your time, I recommend you plan time each week to learn and market yourself. When I maintain a cadence of learning and marketing, I can hone my unique value and make my content marketing even more effective.

I learn by reading and taking workshops. In addition, I engage a coach when I have a thorny problem I don't know how to solve.

Ongoing learning is essential to my success.

13.7.1 Keep Learning

When you become a consultant, you decide how much time and money to invest in your education and training. You will choose how to learn. I like reading and taking workshops, especially if I can work with a cohort.

I recommend you consider these investments in yourself:

- Read business-oriented newspapers such as the *Wall Street Journal* or *The Financial Times* to understand a little more about the world.
- Read periodicals that reflect the state of the art and the practice in your field.
- Read books about consulting, writing, and speaking, so you can improve your consulting skills.

Do you have to buy a library of books on Day One? No. Decide which books you want in which format. And, if you're on a tight budget, take books out of the library and take detailed notes.

However, if you don't read widely, you shortchange yourself and your clients. They will ask you a question about a currently relevant topic, and you won't know anything about it. (Even if you read, you might not know!)

Don't worry if the business book is boring. You might not need to read in-depth—you can scan. However, I read an average of a book a week. I recommend you do, too.

Over the years, people told me they wanted to be a consultant. They wanted advice. I said, "Read these three books and let's talk after you read them." The three books:

- Gerald M. Weinberg's *Secrets of Consulting* WCO14
- Peter Block's *Flawless Consulting* BLO11
- Alan Weiss's *Million Dollar Consulting* WEI16

I chose those three books because they each take a different approach to consulting. In our conversation, I could learn from the would-be consultant's answers.

This small challenge turned into a test of sorts. If they read the books and wanted to discuss the contents, we had a great conversation.

If they didn't want to invest enough in their consulting career to read three books, I knew it wasn't worth my time to discuss consulting with them.

Reading about consulting isn't enough. That's why I recommend you take workshops from other experts. What do they do, and how do they do it? Maybe you can incorporate some of their techniques into your practice. Which workshops will offer you the most value now and later in your career?

13.7.2 *Keep Marketing*

I try to do some form of marketing every day. I tend to write for *daily* marketing. I write any of these: a blog post, a newsletter, an article, part of a book. I write something every day.

I don't always publish every day. I try to publish something at least three times a week. However, life can get in the way, so I commit to *myself* to publish something twice a week. I add this writing to my daily or weekly work. That's part of the consistency in Create Consistent Content.

That consistency means I need to protect my work time.

13.8 Protect Your Work Time

The more successful you are, the more likely people will ask you to take unpaid time away from your work to spend time with them.

I have nothing against an occasional coffee, lunch, or even an informational interview. However, I choose how many meetings I will take, given the commitments I make to *myself.*

My work time includes my content marketing, not just client-specific work. When people ask and I don't have the time, I say no, nicely. I often use the words, "That doesn't work for me."

Sometimes, people request a review of some content, as a way to "give back to the community." That's a request for free work.

Don't let those requests guilt you into doing something that nibbles into your work time

You can say, "No." You don't have to say anything else. For the persistent, I sometimes say, "My time isn't free. No."

Your time is the most valuable resource you have. You can always write another article or speak or deliver a workshop. You can't get time back. That's why I suggested you Set Fees for Writing and Speaking (p. 117).

When you evaluate these requests, decide, and then move on. If the other person is persistent after you said, "No," block them. You don't owe anyone anything.

You owe *yourself* the best business you can build and maintain. Review your calendar. Are you choosing actions that make sense for your business? You can always choose again.

13.9 Now Try This to Manage Your Calendar

None of us has enough time to "do it all." And, we all have the same amount of time in a day. Determine your actions to make choices that work best for your business.

1. Organize the work you want to accomplish for your business this week. As you work through the week, reflect daily and at the end of the week so you can plan for next week.
2. What did you learn this week?
3. What marketing activities did you plan and finish this week?

Make sure you manage your calendar. Don't let your calendar manage you.

In this part, I've suggested you consider how you will create systems to manage everything you can control. But many successful independent consultants choose when to collaborate with others. You can create systems for that collaboration, too.

CHAPTER 14

Collaborate with Other Consultants

I've written this book for your solo practice. And, even as a solo consultant, I've collaborated with others over my career. I've mostly had great experiences because we each brought relatively equal value to the work. And, some engagements were terrible—because we offered unequal value. Sometimes, the other consultant wanted me to take care of his consulting career.

I have two guidelines for collaboration:

- We start at a relatively equal footing.
- We agree on the boundaries of the work and the resulting IP.

Why? Because if we start as relative equals, we don't take care of each other. We work together to create something better than ourselves.

And if we have a contract about the boundaries of our work, especially about the IP, we can relax and do the work.

Here are ways I collaborate with other consultants:

- Refer other consultants to my clients.
- Write with another consultant.
- Present with another consultant.
- Deliver client work with other consultants.
- Create a consulting partnership for some specific outcome.

I've also seen several collaboration traps, which I'll address later in this chapter.

14.1 Refer Other Consultants

Sometimes, I receive inquiries from my current or potential clients—especially about the work I decided to drop. I don't rethink my decision. Instead, I take this opportunity to refer other consultants to the client for that work.

I never refer others for a fee. Ever—either to the client or the consultant. I don't refer for a fee because I don't want to be responsible for the success of the other consultant's work or relationship with that client.

With referrals, I tend to refer three consultants to a client. I stay out of the relationship and urge the client to assess each consultant's value.

Every successful independent consultant makes this choice for him or herself.

I happen to like referring other people to clients or potential clients. I gain several benefits from this:

- Referrals build your network with clients and other consultants.
- The client understands the work I will and will not do. The client remembers me when they have a problem I can solve.
- The client realizes I have an active and extensive network. The client might think of me for better and more work.
- The consultant is happy they didn't have to market for more work.

I don't worry about referral reciprocity. If we all refer work we no longer perform, we all have opportunities to acquire and deliver even better engagements. In addition, your business, the other consultant's business, and the client will gain from your referral.

I don't just refer other consultants. Sometimes, I choose to write with other consultants.

14.2 Write With Other Consultants

Writing is a major part of my content marketing. I've gained several benefits from writing articles with other people:

1. I've learned how other people write. Even if their approach doesn't fit me, I can see what's valuable about their writing style.
2. Each of us brings a different readership. When we write together, we gain introductions to each others' readers.
3. I learn about other perspectives on a given topic.
4. During our conversations while writing, I gain new ideas about the challenges and choices the other consultant sees. My clients benefit from the learning I gain with a co-writer.

I've also written books with other people. Every time I've created a book with someone else, I've gained a more thorough understanding of the topic. And I've gained a new appreciation for other writer's perspectives.

When I write with someone, we both learn together. See Learn with Colleagues (p. 192).

If we place the article on a paid site, we split the royalties right down the middle. That's because I work with people who bring something equal to the relationship.

14.3 Present With Other Consultants

I've had the pleasure of presenting with almost a dozen consultants now. As with writing, we bring each others' audiences to our talks. I learn from how they organize a presentation. And, if we have different styles, the participants can learn from each of us.

I've learned a tremendous amount from public and private talks and workshops with other consultants:

1. Because each of us brings our experience and perspective, the participants can see more alternatives. Sometimes, the other consultant recommends something that has not worked for me—and vice versa. That forces both of us to explain when our recommendations work for us and which do not. That creates a rich workshop experience.

2. Pair-presenting requires more presentation design, including which one of us will do what, and what to do when "something happens" in the moment. And, because we are unique, the audience loves seeing our different perspectives.

3. As we designed, I learned alternative techniques to explain concepts and integrate humor into my presentations. Since presentations are part performance and part education, I'm a better speaker for that learning.

4. Each consultant can reach more people together than they can separately. Especially if you're considering presenting public workshops, you can more easily acquire the minimum number of participants when you speak with another consultant.

5. Working with new people keeps me fresh, and nothing works better for me than positive energy in front of an audience.

I've often learned about designing different activities from my colleagues. That's worth the extra time it takes us to prepare.

When we speak for money, we split the fee right down the middle, the same as with writing together. And when I choose to bring another consultant to work privately with a client, we have a few more items to discuss.

14.4 Deliver Client Work with Others

I limit the number of people in my private and public workshops. That way, I can create the best learning environment for the client. If a client wants more people in a workshop, I increase the fee and ask another consultant to deliver the workshop with me.

I've successfully set the client's and the other consultant's expectations. The other consultant and I agree on these parameters:

- The extent of and the timing for the preparation work we need to create the outcome for the client.
- How we will split the teaching and facilitation responsibilities.
- How we will split the money.

I've collaborated in two ways: where I created the IP and where the other consultant and I co-created the IP.

14.4.1 *Add Another Person to my IP*

Sometimes, clients don't realize how much it costs to bring in another instructor/facilitator for both preparation and delivery time. Sometimes, the results are worth it.

Let's first discuss the costs of bringing in someone else.

Long ago, I taught an experiential workshop, where people practiced and I debriefed their practices. Because of the experiential nature of the workshop, I limited the number of participants to eighteen. But the client wanted thirty people in the workshop.

I suggested they split the workshop into two, with roughly fifteen people in each workshop. No, the client was willing to pay me more than twice my single workshop fee to have everyone in the room.

I asked another consultant, Jim, to work with me to deliver the workshop.

Now, I acted as if I was the agency and Jim was a subcontractor. Here's what I did:

- Asked Jim to sign an NDA.
- Verified Jim's daily rate and the number of days I paid him for. (Two days of preparation and two days of the workshop.) I did not split the money with him evenly.
- We haggled a little over the payment, settling on 50% for him up front, and the remainder when the client paid me.
- Discussed how much Jim could market to the people in the workshop. I asked him to mention his newsletter.
- Finally, we spent two days discussing the workshop and who would facilitate which parts.

We did create a seamless experience for the client. Later, I discovered Jim offered his own workshop—which was a carbon copy of mine.

I was angry, hurt, and disappointed. That was the last time I worked with Jim in any capacity. Not as a volunteer in our professional communities and never with a client.

Your ethics are a part of your brand and unique value. If you don't yet have the IP to "compete" with other consultants, develop your IP as you write, speak, and learn. That's when you'll learn what you really think and how you are different from other consultants.

You don't have to steal anyone's IP.

If you invite other people into your IP, I hope you have a different experience than I had.

However, I've had terrific experiences when we co-create something new.

14.4.2 Co-Create New IP for Clients or Public

I've had the good fortune to co-create workshops with several people. Sometimes, we created something relatively short for a conference. Other times, it was anywhere from two to five days of an intense learning experience.

In the same way that everyone writes or presents differently, everyone creates workshops differently.

I already said that I work with professional equals, so we split the fee down the middle for client or public work.

For public workshops, consider how you want to organize the creation and marketing of your new IP. Here are some possibilities:

- How long will you spend on creating the IP before you start to market it?
- How will each of you market the public event?

When another consultant and I pair to create a workshop, we learn together. We each bring our approach to the content and interactions. I love the co-creation work.

You might want to create a legal partnership, especially if you think you will continue to offer a version of this workshop or event on a periodic basis.

14.5 **Create a Legal Partnership for Longer-Term Events**

While I discuss contracts and partnerships here, I am not a lawyer, and this chapter is not legal advice. Don't create a partnership based solely on this chapter. Hire a lawyer and maybe an accountant. I offer this chapter as a guideline based on my experience.

When I work with a client, they bring the NDA, and the SOW. They might create a Master Service Agreement (MSA), also. It depends on whether you need to register as a vendor with them.

I've never created a legal agreement for a conference talk or a short workshop. That's because we both verbally agreed that we both own the IP. Often, that specific instance of the IP doesn't last past the conference.

However, consider a legal partnership agreement if you plan to collaborate to create longer-term outcomes.

Here are examples of longer-term outcomes:

- Books. Every book is a small business with several possible income streams.
- Conferences. Conferences require a variety of investments, in both time and money. Aside from the time investment, you will incur marketing and venue expenses *before* you can sell registrations.
- Public workshops where several of you collaborate to develop, market, and deliver the workshop.

Your kind of legal agreement will vary depending on the work product. I am not a lawyer, so I can only offer you examples of my choices.

Several of us created and ran the Amplifying Your Effectiveness conference for more than a dozen years. We treated that work as a business because it took us months to market and organize the conference:

- We created a business entity called a Legal Liability Corporation, LLC, to formalize the partnership. That also allowed us to enter into hotel agreements and pay taxes.

- Based on that partnership, we seeded the conference with enough money to start.
- We split the expenses and profits evenly each year.

In contrast, I've offered public two- and three-day workshops with colleagues. Instead of a partnership, we had a one-page agreement that explained we would split all the agreed-upon expenses and profits equally.

When I write books with colleagues, we split the agreed-upon expenses and profits equally. In addition, we each agreed that we would equally own the IP. We could each create our own IP from that book, such as articles, workshops, tutorials, and possibly more books. And, given that the copyright for a book lasts for 70 years past the writer's death, we clarified what will happen when we die.

If you're considering a partnership, clarify the expenses, expectations, and what happens with the IP.

14.5.1 *Clarify the Expenses, Expectations, and Profits Before You Start*

You might not realize the expenses when you start. Here are the costs I've seen:

- Website: Who will host and manage it?
- Marketing: How will you create a mailing list? Who will write the emails? How will people market the partnership efforts? (Will people market themselves or the partnership?)
- Social media might not cost you any money, but someone will need to be responsible for it.

Do you need a corporation for this work? If so, you will need a lawyer, an accountant, and insurance. (See Start Your Business, p. 227, for much more about insurance.)

Clarify the expenses and expectations before you start. I've seen way too many partnerships fumble because one partner wanted the other to take care of too much.

How much do you trust the other person with the work and the clients?

14.5.2 *Make Sure You Trust Your Partners*

How do you know this person is a good partner? I hope you've seen their IP and consulting skills. In addition, you need to trust them with your content and your expectations of how they work.

Only do business with people you trust.

Here's *my* trust checklist for a partnership where we expect longer-term outcomes, such as conferences and books:

1. I trust this person with any of my clients.
2. I trust this person with my intellectual property.
3. I've seen the other person succeed in the effort we're considering for a partnership. For example, the other person understands how to generate content marketing, create and deliver IP, and more.
4. We are both relatively equal as consultants. Both of us have had some success. And I've seen the other person complete and deliver their work in a way that fits my integrity.
5. We have similar goals, including financial goals, for our joint business.
6. As partners, our efforts are worth more to a client than as a solo practitioner.

Consider what you need in your checklist.

You can make partnerships work. Clarify all of these issues—and maybe more. Create a legal document. And, don't forget about what to do when you want to leave the partnership, when someone dies, or when either of you want to dissolve the partnership.

14.5.3 *Clarify the Value*

You might not realize all the value you create with a joint effort. At a minimum, you and your partners have:

- The email list you use to contact potential clients.
- Specific IP for the workshop or book content.
- Sometimes, there's also value in how you organize the event(s).
- The website.

You might have more value, and that's why you need a contract.

14.6 Agree on a Contract

Any extensive collaboration deserves a contract or an agreement. You might call this a "Memo of Understanding." Even in the collaboration traps below, I had written agreements with my fellow consultants.

Even if you shake hands on a verbal agreement, write it down. Make sure both of you understand and agree to your collaboration.

You don't need a contract for when things go well. Contracts help most when you encounter problems. Especially if you create IP together, or build a foundation for the future, what happens when you want to retire? Or, when your partner wants to stop "selling" and wants you to do all the "grunt work?"

Talk everything out. Write the parameters of your agreement down. Both of you sign and date it.

And, remember, as the contracting goes, so goes the contract. If you can't agree on a contract, how can you possibly agree on the outcomes?

I've maintained my solo-by-design approach to my consulting business. And, you might want to create a more permanent relationship with several other independent consultants—all under the umbrella of one corporation. Clarify how you will use the corporation, each person's responsibilities, and when to end the partnership.

14.7 Collaboration Traps

When I collaborate with other consultants, we agree on the work boundaries and the value we each bring to the collaboration.

I've seen these traps when consultants try to collaborate:

- When one consultant takes care of the other. Taking care of people is different from creating better outcomes for a client.
- The primary consultant takes advantage of a subcontractor.
- Ignoring signs your styles don't mesh.

When I work with other consultants, I try to balance everything: our needs and the client's needs. Let me explain why these traps don't work for partnerships.

14.7.1 *One Consultant Takes Care of the Other*

Early in my consulting career, a client wanted to have one large workshop instead of two smaller workshops. I asked another consultant to help me. I thought this other consultant would help me deliver the work.

In exchange for his learning about my IP and the introduction to the client, the other consultant wanted:

- A joint copyright notice, even though he had not created any of the content.
- Half the client fee, even though he had no experience with this client before.
- Marketing meetings with the client.

I made a mistake and agreed to the copyright and fee. I was smart enough to say no to marketing meetings with the client.

I lost money on that engagement. I spent too much time managing the client and the other consultant than I gained in my fee. I'm not sure if anyone received "mutual" benefit in that relationship. And I learned my lesson.

I don't take care of other consultants or clients. Instead, I assume we can all ask for what we want. Just because someone asks doesn't mean I have to give them what they want. I can always say, "No."

Make sure all your agreements create mutual benefit for everyone.

14.7.2 *Primary Consultant Takes Advantage of Subcontractors*

Early in my consulting career, I agreed to subcontract to another consultant. We planned to assess a product development organization. I spent a week, discovered a fundamental problem, and collaborated with the people to create a solution. The primary consultant thought I didn't take enough time. He was worried I collaborated with the client.

He was even more concerned when the client appreciated my part of the assessment more than his part. The primary spent four months and had not discovered the fundamentals necessary for the client's success.

The client asked us to help implement the changes based on my report. Since this was a new engagement, I requested a change in fee. However, the primary consultant was unwilling to increase what he paid me.

In addition, the primary consultant paid me late. That's because the client paid late. I was in the position of reporting to someone who didn't understand the problem, paid me late and inadequately. I declined to take the follow-on engagement.

However, the client wanted to work with me. The primary consultant wanted me to bill through him. I declined that offer, explaining that this engagement was new and separate from the previous agreement.

I learned these lessons from that engagement:

- When working with another consultant, negotiate each phase of the engagement separately. It made sense to have one fee for the assessment and adhere to the primary's reporting style. However, once I worked directly for the client, the old fee and reporting arrangements made no sense.

- Clarify all payments. How fast will the client pay, especially if they pay just one of you? When will the other consultant pay you? If you don't clarify all the payments, the primary might wait for 90 days for the payment. Then the subcontractor waits even longer.
- Make sure all parties believe the arrangements are fair. The client was unhappy about paying money for pieces of an assessment that were not useful. The primary was unhappy because the client saw his work as second-rate. I was unhappy because my fees were too low for the ongoing work, and I had to wait for the primary to bill the client.
- I hadn't recognized the early indications that the primary consultant on the assessment was a controlling personality. If I'd paid closer attention to the pre-engagement activities, I would have recognized the signs and managed our collaboration differently.

If you want to create a successful collaboration, discuss the fee arrangements early, and decide how you'll leverage each other's network.

14.7.3 *Your Styles Don't Mesh*

I didn't realize my style didn't mesh with either colleague in each of these situations. I didn't learn the lesson, "As the contracting goes, so goes the contract."

In a real sense, you create a proposal when working with another consultant. It doesn't matter if you're colleagues or contracting with each other. Look for your style of work and see what happens.

Especially look for secretive plans or work. Look for fairness in the situation—for the other consultant and the client.

14.8 Now Try This for Collaboration

I have enjoyed many of my collaborations.

If you also want to collaborate, consider experiments. For example, when I think about writing a book with a colleague, I start with a small writing collaboration—an article. Can we write together? We need to see how to experiment and succeed with a small effort before considering something much more significant.

As you think about your collaborations, consider experiments.

1. What kinds of collaboration experiments would you consider? Do you want to speak, write, or develop another form of IP with another consultant? For example, you and a colleague might want to create a podcast. You can monetize a podcast. Can you agree on the various circumstances for starting, stopping, monetizing a podcast?
2. What boundaries will you place around the experiment? I almost always start a collaborative writing project with one article.
3. How will you manage fees, client interactions, IP, and more?

Now, it's time to think about how you might start your consulting business so you create a business that works for you.

CHAPTER 15

Start Your Business

There are two parts of starting an independent consulting business:

- Knowing what success means to you, so you create a structure that fits your business.
- The nuts and bolts of creating the business structure.

Let's start with understanding what success means to you

15.1 What Does Success Look Like For You?

There is no One Right Path for successful independent consultants. Each of us defines our success and creates our path, and it all depends on what's important to each of us at the time.

Some people want to be internationally known consultants, traveling worldwide to speak and work. Some people want to work locally or remotely as much as possible to reduce their travel.

Others want what they call a "lifestyle" business, where they attract clients with their content marketing, but they prefer to limit their working hours or the number of active clients.

And maybe you want a business where you work closely with one or two other colleagues.

Only you—with the support of your family—can know what success looks like.

Your definition of success might change as your business grows and evolves. When my children were young, I wanted to stay relatively local. As they grew, I wanted more travel. And in all cases, I wanted fair pay for the value I delivered.

Consider your personal circumstances and the changes you hope to help your clients achieve. Using the possible roles in Figure 1.1: Possible Consulting Roles (p. 4), what does your prospective business look like? That might help you decide to choose from an independent, a two- or three-person, or a firm-based consultancy, where one person sells the work and other people deliver it. You might have some other structure in mind.

For now, let's assume you plan to start an independent consulting business. Start by considering your business structure.

15.2 Structure Your Business for Success

Every business has some form of corporate structure. And while I touch on finances, taxes, and legality in this chapter, none of this chapter is financial or legal advice. Please check everything I say with your country's laws and your financial and legal advisors. I recommend you hire an accountant who understands small businesses.

Now, to get to how you might start.

Remember these tasks I recommended you start back in Build Presence with Active Marketing:

- Online profile.
- Your email address.
- A first draft bio.
- A headshot.
- A business phone number.

I also assume you already have a computer adequate for your needs, a printer with a scanner, and any necessary office supplies.

Now, it's time for these minimum logistics for a successful consulting business:

- A web platform that reflects you: a website with a domain name people can spell. Make sure you have sufficient storage and capacity.
- An email list provider so you can connect with and contact your potential clients.

- Start your social media presence.
- A business phone number.
- A business checking account.
- Appropriate business paperwork as necessary.
- A comfortable and organized place of business.
- Insurance, as risk management for your future.
- Business cards.

Let's walk through these minimum logistics.

15.3 Define Your Web Presence and Email

Everyone researches consultants online. That means you need some sort of website and professional email.

What if you feel like you don't have enough cash to get your own domain and site? Consider starting with a free site and a Gmail address.

There's one caveat to a free site: the provider decides what you can put on your site. Does the service you're considering allow you to add a newsletter signup form on every page of your potential site? Are there other restrictions on what you can create on your "free" site?

Ensure your "free" site offers you the value you need for your business.

If you don't create your site yet, buy your preferred domain name now. When you are ready, you can find an inexpensive hosting service that will allow you to do anything you need for your site.

15.3.1 Choose a Domain Name People Can Spell

You need a domain name that's easy to spell and somehow reminds people of you. That's because your domain name is part of your brand. And, *you* are the brand for your independent consulting practice.

I'm lucky. My name is sufficiently unique and relatively easy to spell. When I bought my domain name, jrothman.com, my first initial and last name were sufficient for a domain name. Since then, I also purchased the domain johannarothman.com so anyone who types that in finds my site.

What if you're not as lucky as I am? Consider your name plus "consultant." For example, janesmithconsultant.com.

I chose my domain name as *my* name, and not my legal business name. No one searching for me cares that my business name is "Rothman Consulting Group, Inc." However, they do want to know about *me*.

If you plan to start a business with one or two colleagues, you'll still need a domain name people can spell, but you might choose some name that's an umbrella name for your business. There are pros and cons to that decision.

The pros for an umbrella name: you don't have to worry about changing the name if people join or leave the business.

The cons are none of the partners' names are part of the domain name.

If you're an independent consultant, should you use some umbrella or aspirational name for your domain name?

Maybe. Consider a name that's not yours under these conditions:

- You have a common name, such as John or Jane Smith, and someone else already bought janesmithconsultant.com.
- You have a name that is too easy to misspell. And, you don't want to buy all the possible misspellings.
- You have a name that sounds "foreign" to the country you want to work most in and is too easy to misspell.

If you decide on an umbrella name, consider how people will know this domain belongs to you. You have some options:

1. Avoid an image with your name, and add your name in plain text on every page of your site.
2. Blog or write articles as often as you can. The more you write, the more you affiliate your name and content with your domain name.

However, an aspirational name requires you fulfill the promise of that name. You might find that difficult, especially as you start your business.

I recommend you learn how to do all of your website setup yourself. I like the ability to change and add to my site when I want to. See *Technical Blogging: Amplify Your Influence, 2nd ed* CAN19 for ideas to start and manage your site.

15.3.2 *Decide on Your Email Name*

I've been jr@jrothman.com since at least 1997. I like having my email reflect my domain name—that's a part of my brand. As I write this, Google is a global driving force. You might prefer or add a Gmail address, such as janesmithconsultant@gmail.com.

Consider an email address such as yourfirstname@yourdomain. com. Everything the client needs to identify you is in your email address.

15.3.3 *Create a Minimum Website*

Since your site helps market you, consider how you can start a relationship with potential clients and colleagues.

Start with these minimum pages for your website:

- A front page that helps potential clients see how you can help them. Start by listing the kinds of problems you help your clients solve. Then, explain how you help solve those problems. ("I offer workshops, online coaching, assessments," as an example.) (See Describe the Signals Your Clients See, p. 17.)
- A signup form for your newsletter on every page. (See Select an Email List Provider, p. 232.)
- An About page, with your bio and your headshot. (See Write a Bio to Attract Clients, p. 58, for more information.)
- A contact form so people can contact you.
- A list of services and products you offer. (See Organize Your Products and Services on p. 157.)

- A newsletter page with back issues of your newsletter so you can Attract Clients With Content Marketing (p. 27).
- A blog page, so you can start your content marketing.

I advise *against* any kind of splash page or animation. Your potential clients are business people who want to solve problems. Don't make them wait to see what you offer.

Avoid any "under construction" section. All websites exist in a state of perpetual construction.

I think about my site as my professional living room. That's where I want to make potential clients feel welcome.

They don't need to see the mess in my office. Or what I'm considering for new products and services. They only need to see what I offer now, my content, and a way to contact me.

Manage Your Site Yourself

When you're starting a business, make sure you can manage your site by yourself. That way, you can add all your content yourself, including your email newsletters.

Start with as simple a site as possible.

Now you have just enough so people can see who you are, how you might serve them, and a way to contact you.

Expect to iterate through your list of pain points and the services and products as you change and evolve your consulting practice.

Now that you have your minimum web presence, consider how you will reach your newsletter subscribers.

15.3.4 *Select an Email List Provider*

Your email list is the single best way to connect with your potential clients. While your social media presence might help, a regular email newsletter will help even more.

See Tammi Labrecque's *Newsletter Ninja: How to Become an Author Mailing List Expert* LAB18 for helpful tips about automation sequences, how often to email your subscribers, and more.

Alternatively, you might want to start with a free newsletter, such as *Substack*.

As your content marketing works, your readers will add themselves to your email list, without you having to do anything except email them regularly.

Don't buy lists of people and their emails for your list. Instead, do everything in Attract Clients With Content Marketing. In addition, mention your newsletter in all of your content and active marketing. On the last slide in each of my presentations, I include a link to my newsletter, my email list. And when I connect with people professionally, I add a little note about my email list.

Those actions offer me organic growth. Since independent consultants don't do everything for everyone, that strategy has helped my "fans" find me. Because I build trust and influence with each newsletter, some of those fans become clients.

Even if you only have one subscriber, use a mailing list provider. That reduces the risk of your client's email provider marking your email address as spam. And when you review email providers, remember to check these two pieces of information:

- What percentage of the emails get through to the people on your list? That's called delivery.
- Does your email provider also access your list, to market to them?

Read the terms of service, another form of legal agreement. Then, write email newsletters at least once a month, adding your copyright to the bottom.

Email newsletters are *your* property. However, social media has a place in your marketing.

15.3.5 *Start your Social Media Presence*

Remember that social media is a form of advertising. Based on their algorithms, these media companies decide how many of your followers will see your posts.

You have no control over who sees your content when you use social media.

That's why I like to think of social media as "renting" space on their platform.

Because you built trust with your readers, you own your list. The platform owns your followers on any given social media. So, sure, use social media, but don't rely on it.

If you can, get your name as your social media handle. And I have found that the more I act as a human being, offering the benefit of the doubt to people, the more likely I am to gain followers. That's my persona, not yours.

Decide the kind of person you want to project in all of your content marketing.

Aside from your web presence, consider how clients can contact you.

15.4 Obtain a Business Phone Number

You can use a cell phone or a separate line for your business number. Do not use your home number because other people might answer that line.

Make sure you have these capabilities on your business line:

- A professional-sounding recording that prompts someone to leave a voicemail.
- Speaker capability so you can type or write and listen simultaneously.
- Headset capability so you can type and listen and possibly record.
- An international calling plan if you plan to discuss work or logistics with people in other countries.

You might choose to use your cell as your business phone. As long as you answer the phone professionally, use anything you want.

15.5 Open a Business Checking Account

In the United States, you might create financial difficulties if you co-mingle business and personal funds. Instead of worrying about which money came from where, open a small business checking account.

Countries tend to tax a business differently than they tax a person's income. You can expect income from:

- Clients who pay you for your services.
- Royalty income from writing.
- Income from products you might sell from your website.

You might wait to open a checking account until you earn some money from a client or your writing, or, you might fund the account with a little bit of money so you can avoid any possible problems.

If you receive royalties or speaking fees, ask your clients to pay your *business* for those services. Even if they make the check out to "Jane Smith," you can still deposit it in your business account.

Money always means paperwork. The paperwork you need will depend on where you live and file taxes.

15.6 File Appropriate Business Paperwork

I am not offering legal advice in this chapter. Please learn your local and national laws about what you need to do to open a business where you live.

In the US, every state and some municipalities have some fingers in your small business. For example, I had to file paperwork in my small town in Massachusetts to conform to the local laws. Otherwise, I would not have a legal business.

Ensure you know the paperwork you need so you file the appropriate business paperwork, including yearly taxes, for your legal business.

Choose Your Business Name

You can name your business anything you want. However, as an *independent* consultant, I recommend you include your name in your business.

When I started my business, I thought I wanted to work with other people, so I named my company, "Rothman Consulting Group." Some of my colleagues use "Their Name and Associates." Both of those are fine and allow you to collaborate with others.

I recommend *against* choosing an aspirational name. Those names sometimes constrain what you choose to offer. Consider a name such as "Reaching Agility Heights." First, there's always a risk that someone wants to trademark two- or three-word phrases. Second, that phrase doesn't differentiate *you* and your value. Third, it constrains you to only agile ways of thinking and working. What if you choose another path?

Name your business what you want, but ask yourself this question: How will people find me online? Use that name.

New consultants often ask me if they should incorporate. You don't have to.

At the current time in the US, you can do everything you need as a DBA, "Doing Business As" entity. That includes opening a business checking account, getting a TIN, a Taxpayer Identification Number, buy business insurance, and probably more I don't know about.

However, assuming you make enough money, I recommend you incorporate. When you incorporate, large companies will accept your incorporation. If you have a DBA business, they will probably make you go through a third party to invoice them.

Always talk to your accountant or lawyer about these decisions.

At this time in the US, there are several forms of corporation. Each has pros and cons for the small business person. While you can incorporate online, always check with your accountant about your expected revenue and which kind of corporation makes the most sense for you.

Nolo Press has many books on business structures.[1] There are pros and cons to every form of business structure. Specifically, consider *Working for Yourself: Law & Taxes for Independent Contractors, Freelancers & Gig Workers of All Types* FIS19.

Do your homework before deciding on a business structure.

15.7 Organize Where You Will Work

Ever since I started my business, I've worked from home in an office with a door. That door allows me a private place to discuss confidential client issues. Even when my children were small, they knew they were not allowed in my office when the door was closed.

I have an ergonomic chair and an ergonomic keyboard, as part of my health. See Manage Your Health (p. 187). If you don't take care of your body, you will not be able to work. You might not need what I do, but make sure your desk and chair are comfortable.

Aside from my physical location, I have several online collaboration, backup, and storage tools. The tools and my office setup allows me enough room and tools to work and collaborate with clients. Make sure you have what you need for successful colleague or client collaboration.

Consider organizing your computer's storage so you can easily find clients, invoices, and email. You might need a different organizational principle for your current and previous IP.

Create an organization that works for you so that you can work effectively. And so you don't have to search while you're on a call with a client. If you say, "I know I had that," you might need a different organization.

---

[1] https://store.nolo.com/products/business-suite/business-formation/starting-a-business

15.8 **Assess Your Insurance Needs**

Everyone needs health insurance. While the need for health insurance is universal, where you live dictates your choices.

In the US, at this writing, you have several options for health insurance:

- As an individual or family, depending on your state.
- Insurance through your spouse or spouse-equivalent.
- Insurance through a professional organization.

My experience is that health insurance is expensive unless you are lucky enough to have your spouse buy the insurance.

Do not scrimp on health insurance. If you're not healthy, you can't consult.

In addition, consider these other business insurance options:

- Errors and Omissions insurance. This insurance protects you if you say something wrong.
- Short-term and long-term disability insurance. Short-term insurance allows you to draw a salary while you can't work if you have a short-term medical problem, such as a knee replacement. Long-term disability protects your income until you are eligible for social security.
- General liability insurance. This kind of insurance protects you if you fall at a client.

Insurance is about managing the risk of you not being able to work. I have all this insurance, and I have not needed much of it. And I'm thrilled I have it because it's much better to have it and not need it than the other way around.

You might think, "I'm young. I don't need long-term disability insurance." Remember, insurance is how you can manage risks for the longer term. Years ago, a colleague was standing on a corner, waiting for the light to change. A car hit him and he suffered a traumatic brain injury.

Overnight, he went from having a thriving business to a place where he had trouble remembering his name. And he didn't have short-term or long-term insurance.

He did sue the insurance company, and lost. He got nothing.

Don't leave your life in other people's hands. You are your independent business. Manage your risks with insurance that works for you.

Every state has different rules about where you can buy insurance. Ask local colleagues who've already started their business. Or, ask your current insurance agent or provider what they offer.

15.9 Print Business Cards

Do you need business cards? Even though you might not give many away, I recommend you do have them.

Consider these items on your business card, as a minimum:

- Your first and last names.
- Your email address.
- Your company name.
- Your website URL.
- Your business phone number.
- Your physical address, if that fits for you.

You might want to add social media information, such as your social media handles or LinkedIn profile URL.

You don't need a logo or branding, because your content marketing is your brand. Even "just" a plain white business card with black ink is fine.

I do not have my physical address on my business cards because I work worldwide. So far, that's not a problem.

I use my local printer to create my business cards. If you use an online service for business cards, make sure you read their terms and conditions. One well-known business card printer now says they have a royalty-free right to use your artwork and create derivative works from your business card.

You've noticed I haven't suggested you spend a lot on infrastructure. That's by design.

15.10 Limit Your Infrastructure Expenses

Many people see new consultants as "easy money." They will charge you a hefty monthly fee for some services because you might not know what you can do yourself. Make sure your fixed monthly expenses are as low as is reasonable—but no lower.

Here's what you don't need:

- A fancy website. Create just the essentials when you start. Avoid buying any services or extras. Start small and as inexpensively as possible.
- An illustrator for graphics. If you need any pictures, take them yourself. Or use royalty-free images. (Verify those images are royalty-free.)
- Anyone who provides you "content" for your site. Write *your* content.
- Editing for your site. Several online apps offer you feedback on your writing. Start with the free app versions.

You don't need a marketing firm to help you get clients. Your clients come to you because of *your* marketing efforts: your writing, your speaking, your emails, your videos, etc. See Attract Clients With Content Marketing.

If you want help with this or anything else in your business, consider these questions:

- How many days of consulting do I need to pay this person for this service? (This is about how you manage ongoing expenses.)
- Is this person or company trying to sell me an ongoing service? That's ongoing retainer work. How many days of consulting do you need every month to pay the person or company?

- How much do you want to work with another person making sure your company survives? I prefer to do most of this myself.

Manage your expenses so you can enjoy your consulting success. See the discussion in Manage Your Money (p. 173).

As you digest all of this, make sure you don't fall into any of these business traps.

15.11 Recognize Consulting Business Traps

Whenever I think I know of all the possible consulting business traps, some enterprising scammer develops another way to make money from existing consultants.

So far, I know of:

- People who will "help" you: find leads, handle your social media, give you a website "in a box." All you have to do is pay them a monthly fee. Forever.
- Artists who will draw you images, including a substitute headshot.

Let me start with the helpers.

15.11.1 Trap: Pay for Helpers

You might feel a little overwhelmed with everything here. Don't let that overwhelm tempt you to pay for someone who will handle your social media and site.

Instead, start small.

Your marketing includes what you post on social media and your site. You are the best at marketing yourself.

You know who your ideal clients are and their concerns. You are the expert for your marketing needs.

If you practice for a while and still think you need help, ask the question I suggested earlier: How many days do you need to work to pay for this service?

15.11.2 *Trap: Pay for Art*

I've heard of too many starving artists. Some of those artists realize they can entice less seasoned or unaware consultants with an offer of art. That art might take several forms: a line drawing instead of a headshot; custom images for pages on your website; or even book covers or custom illustrations for your intellectual property.

I advise against a drawing because the line drawing creates distance between you and the viewer. While the line drawing won't show your receding hairline or my extra chins, will your appearance surprise your clients? Once you start working with a client, they don't notice the hairline or the chins.

What about custom images for your site or book covers? You can use royalty-free stock images from several sites and acknowledge the artist. Alternatively, you can buy royalty-free stock images for a dollar or less per image.

What about custom illustrations for your intellectual property? That's up to you.

I create the image if I think my words need an explanatory image (not a stock photo). As I iterate on the image, I clarify my thinking and the words, and that iteration makes my IP better.

If you decide you need a custom illustration, make sure you have a contract. As part of that contract, define how you can use the image outside of the original use.

Make sure you don't pay for someone else's intellectual property with too many restrictions on how you use that property.

15.12 Now Do This to Start Your Business

My overall guideline is this: Start small and iterate, so you don't spend too much money when you start.

Here's a possible checklist to ensure you have what you need for your business. I'm sure you will want to add or change this list. Consider writing these ideas down in your consulting notebook to review.

The list:

1. An online home for your website and a place for your newsletter archive.
2. An email newsletter provider that will manage subscribers.
3. A phone.
4. A business bank account.
5. Filed all necessary paperwork to legally work as a business in your town, state, and country.
6. A comfortable and organized place of business, so you want to go to work every day.
7. Enough insurance to manage risks, both personal and professional.
8. Business cards.

You've got the basics now. You know what success looks like for you, how to manage your calendar, the value you offer your clients, and how to start a business.

Now that you know what you need to start your business, it's time to consider evolving and adapting as you proceed.

CHAPTER 16

Adapt and Evolve Your Successful Practice

In Part 1 of this book, you saw how to initiate and build the client relationship so both you and the client gain mutual benefit. The consultant offers valuable expertise the client wants. And the client experiences the benefit of some change or transformation.

Many of us find it's easier to see and support other people's transformation than our own. Why should you change, especially if your consulting practice is doing well?

If consultants expect their clients to change, consultants might choose to change, too. Especially if the consultant experiences both financial and professional success.

I've changed my offerings and problems to solve several times over the course of my consulting career. Partly, I chose to build new income streams. But, sometimes, I got bored with my previous offerings.

You might get lucky and have a long and fulfilling consulting career without changing anything. As a consultant, I've met only two consultants who did *not* change their offerings. They were fortunate— they had enough clients until they retired. (Their offerings no longer have a place in our current environment.)

More of us change our business model as we gain more experience to maintain our business resilience.

I prefer to change on my terms, not someone else's. That's why I choose to adapt, even before the market vanishes.

16.1 **Choose to Adapt Your Practice**

I've seen many reasons to adapt my practice:

- Clients change—they change what they need and when they need it.
- Since I've learned and created new IP, I can take advantage of that new IP.
- Society changes. What worked before doesn't work anymore.

Let's start with the clients.

16.1.1 *Clients Change*

My experience says industries change at least once every decade. During that decade, clients realize they have different problems. They no longer want to buy those tried-and-true (same) products and services you offer. They want something different. Even if your IP and work is *still* relevant, clients want something new.

Sometimes, the clients have new problems. Their old problems vanished.

Other times, the client needs a new approach. Or, they've heard about a different approach and they want you to use that new approach.

In this case, you might need to change your ideal clients or how you present your products or services.

Because you have your perspective on your various expertise and how to apply it, you don't have to predict the future. Instead, continue to create new IP, using the Figure 3.1: Interplay Between Writing and Speaking (p. 32).

As you create new IP, that IP helps you change a little bit at a time.

16.1.2 *Change With New Intellectual Property*

My clients often see what I can offer them before I do. That's one of the values of continuing to create new IP. A client sees a blog post or newsletter, and asks for a discovery call. As we talk, we can explore alternatives I might not have considered before.

My thought leadership/provocation doesn't just help my clients—it helps me, too.

Successful independent consultants use their new IP to move from possible commodity work, and redefine how they can make money.

Even better, consultants continue to learn as they create new IP.

However, there's at least one more good reason to change: sometimes, the entire world changes.

16.1.3 Adapt When Society Changes

Financial events, such as recessions change society. So do pandemics. The COVID-19 pandemic created much more opportunity—and demand—for online work than we ever experienced before.

That's why it's worth your time to consider how you can practice changing your business before the world changes your business for you.

16.2 Practice Changing Your Business Model

In Assess Your Business Model Over Time (p. 170), I said I ask questions about all my offerings every year. As you change your practice, consider which clients will select which products and services. Which offerings or clients should you keep, drop, or change?

What if you start with a small change, changing your clients?

One consultant, who focused on project management, told me this story:

"Up until the Great Recession of 2007-2008, I focused on projects for banks and other financial organizations. Then, *all* my work dried up just before Christmas in 2007. All my clients canceled all my work.

"It wasn't just me. All the internal people were hustling for new jobs. They offered workshops literally for grocery money. I could not compete. My business was in big trouble.

"Then, a client who lost her job at a bank started an online shopping business. She remembered me because of my monthly newsletter. She offered me work, and wow, did I need it. Once I finished that three-month engagement, I leveraged that work into more work. Yes, I asked for referrals.

"That taught me the value of a resilient business with multiple kinds of clients. I still focus on projects, but I don't focus on only one industry. My practice is more resilient."

You don't have to wait for an entire industry to vanish. Instead, assess your revenue sources every month, quarter, and year. See how varied your revenue streams and clients are. Then, you can decide what to do.

Because I want variety in what I do, I choose what to change and when. My updated IP helps me update or create new workshops or coaching or consulting, because my clients see what I'm writing and speaking about now. That allows me to drop some percentage of my previous work every year.

That's how I evolve my business.

The more IP you can offer—even if you focus that IP narrowly—the more you can create a resilient business. You can adapt and evolve your business before you need to.

16.3 The Market Decides When You Change

Sometimes, the market decides when you should change your business.

For example, I happily taught my older project management workshop in 2008. By 2009, no one wanted that original workshop—even though my clients would have discovered a better path to agility with that workshop.

How did I prepare for a new workshop? I started teaching new material in 2007, mainly as a bridge for my clients. By the time demand for the old workshop disappeared, I had a new workshop to take its place. I used content marketing to let people know I offered the new workshop.

As a guideline, consider dropping 10–15% of your business every 12–18 months.

In the case of my project management workshop, I didn't have time to consider what to do. The market decided for me and fast.

Sometimes, the world changes, and you react, such as with the pandemic. Several of my consulting colleagues only knew how to travel to clients to deliver products and services. Since I wanted to travel less, I'd started offering online workshops back in 2012. (I wince when I look back at them.)

I want to choose when and what to change in my business. When we decide when to adapt and evolve, we can make better decisions than when the world decides.

And that includes our business systems.

16.4 Decide What Change Means for Your Business

While I do recommend you change what you offer and how, ask yourself if your systems still work for you.

James Clear, in *Atomic Habits* CLE18 said it perfectly:

"You do not rise to the level of your goals. You fall to the level of your systems."

Assess your consulting engine, especially how you create content and where you place it. If you've been writing a lot, maybe it's time to consider video. If you've mastered video and speaking, maybe consider writing or podcasting.

While I don't tend to change my exercise routine, plenty of my colleagues do like to change their exercise and the foods they eat. And the same thinking applies to how you manage your calendar and choose actions.

I do experiment with new systems on a regular basis, even if those systems don't address my health or my calendar.

My systems are part of my purposeful change.

16.5 Evolve Your Practice Purposefully

You might have had a terrific business model, and then something changed. As I wrote this book during the COVID-19 pandemic, too many consultants had one income stream: offer in-person workshops almost anywhere globally. Maybe they had a book or two, also. But, the bulk of their revenue came from in-person workshops.

They needed to change and change fast. Most of these consultants did, but they had to react to forced change.

I want to choose my changes, not react to change. That's why I've used the idea of "drop some percentage" of your business every year.

That's also why I don't give the same talk at every conference.

I change my products and services every year. In addition, I assess and adapt my systems every year.

While I continue my strategy of a monthly newsletter, I've changed tactics. I've lost count of the number of newsletter providers I've used. I learned to use various tools as I did more remote work—and I enjoy them. I realized that I could create better outcomes as I changed my tactics.

I become a better consultant when I change my practice and my systems.

That's what I wish for you, too. To improve your practice and your business of consulting. And maybe that means consulting isn't for you, at least not yet.

16.6 Consulting Is Not for You—Yet

Is consulting for you?

Maybe you've read this book, done the homework, and decided independent consulting isn't for you, at least not now.

You might decide you want to focus on learning more as an employee. Or that you want to take some classes to acquire unique expertise.

I recommend you start to write and speak now. You can build your content and your expertise as you work.

Keep learning. Build and experiment with your learning cohort. You will create *your* great career. Isn't that the point?

My best to you on your journey.

Evaluate Your Technical Skills

How will you help your clients change or transform to achieve better results? In Chapter 1, Define Your Unique Value (p. 3) I offered an introduction to skills you need as a consultant.

Now, it's time to inventory your skills to think about the kind of consultant you want to be and where you are now. Start with your technical skills.

Understand All Your Technical Skills

We have a variety of expertise—specifically, our technical and non-technical skills. Each of these various skills offers potential value to our clients.

First, we each have technical skills. In *Hiring Geeks That Fit* ROT12, I suggest there are four kinds of technical skills:

- Functional skills: how we perform a specific role.
- Product domain expertise: how we acquire product or client knowledge.
- Tools and technology expertise.
- Industry experience.

Here's how I explain each of these four sets of technical skills.

Functional Skills

Functional skills are how you perform a specific role. These skills are technology- and tool-independent.

If you're a technical coach for software teams, you might have functional skills in domain-driven design, or test-driven development, or test automation. You understand—at a deep level—what developers or testers do and their concerns.

Maybe you're a product person. You have functional skills around eliciting requirements, organizing backlogs and roadmaps, and planning with a team. You understand how product planning can help or hurt both the team and the product.

Maybe you're a facilitator. You understand various kinds of meetings—how to organize them, keep them on track, and which type of meetings work for which problems.

As a consultant, you need the ability to see, describe, and reason about the client's current state and how you might support their changes.

Consider these functional skills also: management, customer support, or marketing.

What kind of deep functional skills do you have?

Product Domain Expertise

I like to consider two kinds of product domain expertise: problem-space and solution-space.

Problem-space domain expertise focuses on the problems the organization has in creating, selling, and delivering its products to the customer or buyer. Problem-space expertise focuses on the why and what questions.

Solution-space domain expertise focuses on how the organization creates, sells, and delivers its products. Often, solution-space expertise requires you to learn the intimate technical details.

The more expertise you have, the more questions you can ask about who the customers are and when the customers need or want the product or service.

With solution-space expertise, you can see and reason about causes, effects, and possible interventions. You can see or create visualizations about how the product or the organization works—or doesn't.

Armed with that knowledge, you can propose interventions or experiments or other changes for your clients.

That means the more experience you have, the faster you can see how patterns in your previous work can apply to this new client. Imagine you've been a product manager in both IT and Engineering organizations, for both software and hardware products. That's cross-industry expertise (hardware and software, plus IT and Engineering.)

That expertise means you can offer more value to your clients. You can explain how you've seen their challenges in other industries. Your clients do not see you as a commodity, but as someone who can add more value to the consulting relationship.

While I prefer to have cross-industry expertise, you might prefer to have a more vertical focus. As long as no client sees you as a commodity, you can choose how to focus your work. See the discussion in Decide How You Will Make Money (p. 157).

Consider how you see your clients' problems. How fast can you understand the problem space? What knowledge are you missing so you can't easily see possible solution-space ideas for your clients?

Tools and Technology Expertise

You might have a certification in a specific security tool. Or in how to use a particular piece of software.

Or, you might limit your clients to those people with WordPress concerns or Linux challenges.

Tools and technology expertise requires in-depth knowledge of the tool or technology. Beware of becoming a commodity if you focus *only* on tools and technology.

Industry Expertise

You might have years of experience in the banking, insurance, or pharmaceutical industry. (You might choose a different industry that's more relevant to you.) And you want to stay in that industry. Add those skills to your skills inventory.

You don't just have these technical skills. The next appendix offers several ways to think about your "consulting tools" as you reason about your client's challenges.

Consider These Consulting Tools

Consultants need ways to visualize and describe the client's system, to identify the problems and the options to solve those problems, and then communicate with the client.

Those are consulting "tools," for lack of a better name.

You might already be familiar with many of these ideas. However, some of my technical reviewers didn't realize they already knew and used many of the "tools" in this Appendix. And some of my reviewers were unaware of these options.

If these ideas are new to you, first do an online search and see how other people use them. Then create a reading list for yourself and read and experiment more.

Let's start with how to see the client's reality.

See the Client's Reality

Every organization has its own system and culture. The culture creates feedback loops and often causes the problems the client sees. What the client sees is a signal, not necessarily the problem itself.

The problems arise because of the system. The physician Dr. Paul Batalden was correct when he said:

"Every system is perfectly designed to get the results it gets."

The more you can see—and help the client see—their system, the more opportunities you have to create useful interventions and support the client's changes.

Here are two questions about reality I find quite useful:

- What do you see and hear? This question helps ground the client and the consultant in the client's reality.
- What would you like to see and hear? This question helps the client articulate the outcomes and the possible future.

Since clients often see the *signals*, but not the root causes of the problems, you might need more tools to reason about the current reality.

Reasoning Tools

These are just a few of the reasoning tools available.

- Force Field Analysis, which I mentioned back in Chapter 1. Developed by Kurt Lewin in the 1940s. There are plenty of descriptions online. One is at Mindtools.[1]
- Balancing and Reinforcing feedback loops: The screech you hear from a microphone that reinforces the sound is a reinforcing feedback loop. Thermostats use balancing feedback loops to prevent a lot of change. If you want to know more, start with *The Fifth Discipline: The Art & Practice of The Learning Organization* by Peter Senge, or *Business Dynamics: Systems Thinking and Modeling for a Complex World* by John D. Sterman, McGraw Hill/Irwin, 2000.
- Concept maps can help people understand how they link information in their organization.[2]
- Connection circles to understand the various causes, effects, and the relationships between each of them.[3]

---

[1] https://www.mindtools.com/pages/article/newTED_06.htm

[2] https://cmap.ihmc.us/docs/theory-of-concept-maps.php

[3] https://thesystemsthinker.com/learning-about-connection-circles/

This is not an exhaustive list of ways to visualize and reason about systems. How will you see each client's context and explain that context to those people?

In addition to these named tools, consider laws, principles, and anecdotes to guide your thinking

Use Laws and Principles to Guide Your Thinking

Here are some laws:

- Murphy's Law and its corollary: Whatever can go wrong will, at the worst possible time.
- Goodhart's Law: When a measurement becomes a target, it ceases to be a good measure.
- Hofstadter's Law: Everything takes longer, even when you take Hofstadter's Law into account.
- Parkinson's Law: Work expands to fill the time allotted.

Some principles:

- The Peter Principle: People get promoted to their level of incompetence.
- What got you here won't get you there. Marshall Goldsmith wrote a book by that name, and just the name is a principle you can use.
- Occam's Razor: the simplest explanation is often the correct one.
- The definition of insanity: continuing the same actions and expecting different results.

Your clients are human, so they (and you!) will encounter these principles.

You might even see some actions or consequences at your client that remind you of a fable. Use that story as a basis for your description for the client.

Once we can see the system, we can identify candidate problems and solutions.

Problem-Solving Tools

Consider these tools as a way to frame the problems you see:

- The Cynefin[4] framework to help you see possibilities to organize your suggestions to the client. Clients can solve the simple problems themselves. But the complicated or complex problems? That's when they call consultants. The complex problems require experiments to solve—and consultants can shine there.

- The OODA loop: Observe, Orient, Decide, Act. John Boyd, a fighter pilot in World War II developed this concept. Because of its feedback loops, it's a great way to consider alternatives for solving problems. I enjoyed the biography: *Boyd: The Fighter Pilot Who Changed the Art of War* by Robert Coram.

- The Eisenhower two-by-two matrix that helps people differentiate importance and urgency. Even if clients "know" this already, you might use the matrix to help them reason through their data.

- Ladder of Inference from Senge's *The Fifth Discipline* helps us realize how much real data we have and how we've applied it.

- Wardley Maps[5] show you where you might innovate and where innovation might not be useful.

In addition, I use the organizational mapping technique from Weinberg's *Experiential Learning 2: Inventing* WEL12 to ask the client to draw the system.

Once we see and reason about problems, we might need to see data.

---

[4] https://thecynefin.co/

[5] https://learnwardleymapping.com

Data Gathering and Visualization Tools

Sometimes, consultants need to reason about the problem before they can decide which data to collect. Other times, consultants collect some data and then reason about the problem. There is no One Right Way to assess what's happening with the client.

That said, most consultants need to gather both qualitative and quantitative data to aid their clients in making sense of the situation.

Value stream maps are one way to gather *both* kinds of data in one place. A value stream map shows the current flow of work and how long it takes to perform each step of the work. Once the client sees the work time, the wait time, and the total time, they are more apt to consider your suggestions.

I also use:

- Time series, when the data depends on what's happening over a time period.
- Histograms, control charts, and other ways to visualize data.
- Mean, median, mode to make sense of related but disparate data.

I have not yet had to run regressions or otherwise use what I would call "advanced" data capabilities. I have used spreadsheets to help the client see what's going on.

Two-by-two matrices help people compare and contrast to create valuable outcomes. I already suggested Eisenhower's matrix. I offered the Business Model Axes matrix in Figure 10.1: Business Model Axes (p. 158). You can also create two-by-two matrices to support people as they think through what might be opposing issues.

I often use the Pareto Principle, also known as the 80/20 rule, when discussing what causes problems for my clients. That's because a few root causes create many of the signals the client sees.

Given your expertise, you might gather other kinds of data. Consider using reinforcing and balancing feedback loops to guide your data collection. For example, in software development, the Fault Feedback Ratio is an indicator of how many problems the team can't fix and keep fixed. The problems keep arising. That's based on a variety of feedback loops.

Master Your Industry Frameworks

You might have mastered several frameworks in your industry, regardless of whether you have a certification in that framework. Even if a professional organization offers a framework or certification, you probably don't need one—unless you need a license to practice.

I hope those frameworks remain relevant throughout your career. In my experience, industry frameworks change at least once a decade. And too often, mastering those frameworks leads to commodity work.

However, you might need a *license* to do your work. Some examples are:

- Professional Engineer
- CPA, Certified Public Accountant

As you consider your consulting "tools," consider principles that remain constant throughout your career. You can add value to your work by applying those principles to your client's challenges.

Annotated Bibliography and Recommended Reading

[ALL15] Allen, David. *Getting Things Done: The art of stress-free productivity*. Penguin, 2015. I was lucky enough to take a seminar from David back in the early 90s. Since then, I've used his ideas to plan my next actions, not attempt to manage my time.

[BEN11] Benson, Jim and Tonianne DeMaria Barry. *Personal Kanban: Mapping Work | Navigating Life*. CreateSpace, 2011. This is the book that really explains how to use personal kanban in an easy-to-understand way. I read the book, internalized it, and did not realize that I was quoting from it. That's how easy it is to understand, internalize, and adopt personal kanban. You can drop the personal from that sentence, too, and apply the principles as kanban in projects at work.

[BLO11] Block, Peter. *Flawless Consulting: A Guide to Getting Your Expertise Used, 3rd ed.* Pfeiffer. San Francisco. A classic in the consulting field.

[CAN19] Cangiano, Antonio. *Technical Blogging: Amplify Your Influence, 2nd ed.* Pragmatic Bookshelf. 2019. Not just blogging, but includes everything you need to create and manage an effective website.

[CKM90] Champion, Douglas P., David H. Kiel, and Jean A. McLendon. *Choosing a Consulting Role: Principles and Dynamics of Matching Role to Situation*. In *Training & Development Journal*, February 1990. I always knew there were several possible stances as a consultant. This paper explains the whys and whens of each stance.

[CLE18] Clear, James. *Atomic Habits: An Easy & Proven Way to Build Good Habits & Break Bad Ones.* Penguin Random House, 2018.

[CSI08] Csikszentmihalyi, Mihaly. *Flow: The Psychology of Optimal Experience.* HarperCollins Publishers, 2008. Learn how people finish work, separately and together.

[DIB16] Dib, Allan. *The 1-Page Marketing Plan: Get New Customers, Make More Money, And Stand Out From The Crowd.* Successwise, 2016.

[DWE07] Dweck, Carol. *Mindset: The New Psychology of Success.* Ballantine Books, New York, 2007. This book discusses the fixed mindset and the growth mindset. If you have the fixed mindset, you believe you can only do what you were born with. If you have the growth mindset, you believe you can acquire new skills and learn. The growth mindset allows you to improve, a little at a time.

[DRU73] Drucker, Peter. *Management: Tasks, Responsibilities, Practices.* Harper Collins. 1973. Originally published in 1973 with reprints in 1985 and 1993, I consider this the bible of what modern management should be. If you're put off by his language, please read past his use of "man" as the only gender for manager. Us modern readers can substitute "people" for the word "man" and the content is as fresh and useful as it was back when Drucker first published the book.

[FIS19] Fishman, Stephen J.D. *Working for Yourself: Law & Taxes for Independent Contractors, Freelancers & Gig Workers of All Types,* 11th ed. Nolo Press. 2019. A US focus for types of business structures. Quite useful for framing your thinking, regardless of where you work in the world.

[FIS17] Fishman, Stephen. *The Copyright Handbook: What Every Writer Needs to Know.* Nolo Press. 2017. Fishman updates this book regularly. This is the version I own and refer to on a regular basis.

Buy one. Read it. Search inside for various scenarios. Learn to protect your IP and exploit it.

[FRE09] Fredrickson, Barbara. *Positivity: Top-Notch Research Reveals the 3-to-1 Ratio That Will Change Your Life*. Harmony Books, 2009. Positivity isn't about "being happy." Instead, this book helps you see how you can create a more positive environment for *yourself*. You don't need to depend on other people to create a positive life.

[GOD18] Godin, Seth. *This Is Marketing: You Can't Be Seen Until You Learn to See*. You don't have to be an intuitive or "gifted" marketer to be effective. All you need is this book and to integrate all the ideas within it. You might also want to read all of Godin's other books and his blog, because everything he writes relates to marketing.

[LAB18] Labrecque, Tammi L. *Newsletter Ninja: How to Become an Author Mailing List Expert*. larks & katydids. 2018. Yes, the title says "author" and this book works perfectly for consultants.

[LUC20] Lucas, Michael W. *Cash Flow for Creators: How To Transform your Art Into a Career*. Tilted Windmill Press. 2020. I never thought I would laugh out loud at a book about money. Cash flow really is a game, and Lucas excels (small pun) at describing the game and how to win.

[KAH11] Kahneman, Daniel. *Thinking Fast and Slow*. Farrar, Straus and Giroux. 2011. Many of us (including me) think we understand how we think. Not so fast. In this classic text, learn all the various thinking traps and fallacies.

[MIH85] Miller, Robert B. and Stephen Heiman. *Strategic Selling: The Unique Sales System Proven Successful by America's Best Companies*. William Morrow, 1985. I first learned about the various buyers in 1988 and it totally changed how I thought of allies and people I perceived as obstacles. If you want to sell anything, read this book.

[PFE10] Pfeffer, Jeffrey. *Power: Why Some People Have It and Others Don't.* New York: HarperCollins, 2010. I don't agree with everything Pfeffer says, but he always makes me think. I do agree with what he says about networking. Like I said, he makes me think. He'll make you think, too.

[ROT12] Rothman, Johanna. *Hiring Geeks That Fit.* Practical Ink, 2012. Learn to hire people, from writing a job description to a great first day. All the templates are available for free on Johanna's website. The book explains how to use them.

[ROT16] Rothman, Johanna. *Manage Your Project Portfolio: Increase Your Capacity and Finish More Projects, 2nd ed.* Pragmatic Bookshelf, Dallas, TX and Raleigh, NC, 2016. This book helps you visualize, choose, and manage all the work in your project portfolio. I wrote it for larger companies, and it works just as well for one-person companies.

[ROT22] Rothman, Johanna. *Free Your Inner Nonfiction Writer: Educate, Influence, and Entertain Your Readers.* Practical Ink, 2022. Specifically for shorter nonfiction, such as you would use in content marketing.

[SEL06] Seligman, Marty. *Learned Optimism: How to Change Your Mind and Your Life.* Vintage Books. 2006. I discovered, I am an optimist by nature. And, when I'm not, I learned several ways to regain my optimism. You will learn more about yourself than you imagined.

[SHE97] Shenson, Howard and Ted Nicholas. *The Complete Guide to Consulting Success,* 3rd ed. Upstart Publishing Company. 1997. The principles remain as useful now as when I read the original three-ring binder version back in 1994.

[SMI17] Smith, Dean Wesley. *The Magic Bakery.* WMG Publishing. 2017. Written for fiction writers, it's just as applicable to non-fiction writers. In fact, since non-fiction writers might write more articles than books, it's even more important for non-fiction writers to learn how to exploit their IP rights.

[WEL12] Weinberg, Gerald M. *Experiential Learning 2: Inventing.* Aside from organizational mapping, this book (and the others that are part of the same series) offers consultants many ways to see the system. Based on what people see, consultants and clients can consider alternative actions.

[WCO14] Weinberg, Gerald M. *The Secrets of Consulting: A Guide to Giving and Getting Advice Successfully.* 2014. An excellent book for understanding what consulting is—and is not.

[WCM14] Weinberg, Gerald M. *More Secrets of Consulting: The Consultant's Toolkit.* 2014. All about self-esteem.

[WEI93] Weinberg, Gerald M. *Software Quality Management, Vol 2: First-Order Measurement.* Dorset House Publishing, New York, 1993. This particular Weinberg book has excellent definitions of congruence and human interaction.

[WEI16] Weiss, Alan. *Million Dollar Consulting: The Professional's Guide to Growing a Practice,*5th ed. McGraw Hill. 2016. I've learned a tremendous amount from Weiss throughout the years. I've adapted his proposal template and how to structure fees based on what I learned from him.

Other books you might enjoy:

Grahl, Tim. *Your First 1000 Copies: The Step-by-Step Guide to Marketing Your Book,* 2nd ed. Story Grid Publishing. 2020. While Grahl markets this book to writers, the book is equally effective for any information-based product. Since consultants offer information, I found this book useful for marketing my business.

Laborde, Genie. *Influencing with Integrity.* Crown House Publishing. Wales, 1998. Laborde offers a comprehensive approach to influence where each person gains something. Useful for internal consultants and necessary for external consultants.

Siebert, Al. *The Resiliency Advantage: Master Change, Thrive Under Pressure, and Bounce Back from Setbacks.* Berrett-Koehler Publishers, Inc. San Francisco. 2008. Siebert claims we have five levels of resiliency: Physical, problem solving, inner selves, curiosity, and synergy. You might be surprised at what you learn about yourself from this book.

More from Johanna

People know me as the "Pragmatic Manager." I help leaders and teams see simple and reasonable alternatives that might work in their context—often with a bit of humor. Equipped with that knowledge, they can decide how to adapt how they work.

If you liked this book, you might also like the other books I've written:

Management Books:
- Practical Ways to Manage Yourself: Modern Management Made Easy, Book 1
- *Practical Ways to Lead and Serve—Manage—Others: Modern Management Made Easy, Book 2*
- *Practical Ways to Lead an Innovative Organization: Modern Management Made Easy, Book 3*
- *Behind Closed Doors: Secrets of Great Management*
- *Hiring Geeks That Fit*

Product Development:
- *From Chaos to Successful Distributed Agile Teams: Collaborate to Deliver*
- *Create Your Successful Agile Project: Collaborate, Measure, Estimate, Deliver*
- *Manage Your Project Portfolio: Increase Your Capacity and Finish More Projects, 2nd ed*
- *Agile and Lean Program Management: Scaling Collaboration Across the Organization*

- *Diving for Hidden Treasures: Uncovering the Cost of Delay Your Project Portfolio*
- *Predicting the Unpredictable: Pragmatic Approaches to Estimating Project Cost or Schedule*
- *Project Portfolio Tips: Twelve Ideas for Focusing on the Work You Need to Start & Finish*
- *Manage It!: Your Guide to Modern, Pragmatic Project Management*

Personal Product Development:
- *Free Your Inner Nonfiction Writer*
- *Successful Independent Consulting*
- *Write a Conference Proposal*
- *Manage Your Job Search*

I'd like to stay in touch with you. If you don't already subscribe, please sign up for my email newsletter, the Pragmatic Manager, on www.jrothman.com.

Please do invite me to connect with you on LinkedIn, follow me on Twitter, @johannarothman, or follow me on Mastodon, https://mastodon.sdf.org/@johannarothman.

See my workshops page for future consulting cohorts.

Did this book help you? If so, please consider writing a review of it. Reviews help other readers find books. Thanks!

—Johanna

Index

www.ingramcontent.com/pod-product-compliance
Lightning Source LLC
Chambersburg PA
CBHW061204220326
41597CB00015BA/1422